Life, Love and
The Archers

WENDY COPE

Life, Love and The Archers

Recollections, reviews and other prose

www.tworoadsbooks.com

First published in Great Britain in 2014 by Two Roads
An imprint of John Murray Press
An Hachette UK company

1

A CIP catalogue record for this title is available from the British Library

Hardback ISBN 978 1 444 79536 3
Ebook ISBN 978 1 444 79535 6

Typeset in Sabon LT Std by Palimpsest Book Production Limited,
Falkirk, Stirlingshire

Printed and bound by Clays Ltd, St Ives plc

Hodder & Stoughton policy is to use papers that are natural, renewable
and recyclable products and made from wood grown in sustainable forests.
The logging and manufacturing processes are expected to conform to the
environmental regulations of the country of origin.

Hodder & Stoughton Ltd
338 Euston Road
London NW1 3BH

www.hodder.co.uk

To Lachlan

CONTENTS

Introduction

I Remember

Education, Education

A Nice, Polite Patient

A Man in One's Life

A Mark on a Piece of Paper

Addictions, Ageing and Two Cathedral Cities

Head in a Book

Settee Life

Life, Love and
The Archers

Introduction

I had just done a poetry reading in a school and it was time for questions. In response to one pupil I had explained that there had been long periods when I didn't produce any poems and was afraid I might never do so again. A girl put her hand up: 'If you can't make up any more poems, would you think about trying to be a writer?'

Very politely, I explained that I was a writer already. I had written several books of poems.

Her mistake is quite a common one. You often see people described as 'poet and writer', which is a bit like saying someone is a woman and a person.

Anyway, here is a volume that is indisputably a book of writing, although it does include two or three poems. Some of it was written during one of the periods referred to above, when I didn't have any ideas for poems. To give myself something to do, I embarked on an autobiography. This wasn't a serious attempt to write a publishable book. If it had been, I probably wouldn't have been able to write much at all. It was a question of giving it a whirl and seeing what happened. This was some time in the early noughties. I wrote more than 30,000 words before abandoning the project at the point in the story where I went to university. I couldn't face writing about that. There's a piece in here entitled 'On Failure' that touches on the problem.

The memoir stayed in a folder on my computer until 2011, when I sold my archive to the British Library. It was discovered there by Lisa Highton, my editor, when she went, with my permission, to look through the archive for publishable material.

She thought parts of it were fit to be in a book, if I did some revising. One small part of that work was to change a few names, as any readers who were at school with me will notice. She found other things too. The most surprising, to me, was a short story called 'Ladies Do Not Rescue Princes'. I had completely forgotten about that. She also found some articles I'd written but never attempted to publish: the piece on smoking, for example, and the one about Billy Graham.

The extracts from the memoir mostly appear in the first two sections of the book. Much of the rest was commissioned for publication. It is well known that Cyril Connolly, in his book *Enemies of Promise*, warned that 'the pram in the hall' is one of those enemies. Another of the enemies, Mr Vampire, is less well known. Mr Vampire is the editor who tempts promising writers into journalism. One idea I had for the title of this book was 'Working for Mr Vampire'. The publishers weren't keen and it did seem unfair on the editors who commissioned these pieces. They gave me paid work when I needed it. And several of them were very encouraging and patient with a writer who didn't have much confidence. Nicholas Shakespeare and John Coldstream, formerly of the *Daily elegraph*, Charles Moore, former editor of the *Spectator*, and Craig Raine, editor of *Areté*, all deserve special thanks for believing in my ability to write. They continue to be some of my favourite people.

Thanks, too, to Lisa Highton of Two Roads, whose enthusiasm and drive made this book happen. I am very lucky indeed to have an editor who was willing to go rooting around in boxes in the British Library to find publishable work that might have remained hidden there for ever. And to my agent Carol MacArthur, for her part in persuading me that the project was a good idea.

I was very pleased when the talented young artist, Jon McNaught, whose work I have admired for several years, agreed to do the cover and some illustrations for this book. And I am very pleased with his pictures.

This is not the first time I have finished an introduction with a paragraph about my husband, the poet and critic Lachlan Mackinnon. He has devoted a lot of time and energy to this book, egging me on, calming my anxieties, reading and rereading all of it and making helpful suggestions. I cannot thank him enough.

May 2014

I Remember

The first piece in this book was commissioned by Craig Raine, editor of Areté *magazine, for a feature called 'Homage to Joe Brainard'. Brainard was a New York painter, who died in 1994. He wrote a book entitled* I Remember, *in which, according to Raine's introduction, 'Each entry begins with the words "I remember" and their authority is based on truth.' Other contributors to the same issue (18, Autumn 2005) included the actress Harriet Walter, authors David Lodge, Patrick Marber and Sue Townsend, and TV presenter Anne Robinson. I often use the 'I remember' idea on writing courses to help people get going. It never fails.*

I Remember the First Time
I Read a Book by Myself

I remember the first time I read a book by myself. It was *The Buttercup Farm Family* by Enid Blyton. I got stuck on the word 'put' and had to ask Nanna.

I remember getting angry with my sister and sitting on top of her and banging her head on the floor.

I remember sitting at the piano making up a tune, then thinking it couldn't be any good because to do it properly you had to have lessons in composing.

I remember a frightening dream about being chased by Captain Hook and the pirates.

I remember when we kept chickens in the back garden and I collected the eggs.

I remember being told to write a poem at school when I was six. I didn't know how to begin, so I copied the first line from the girl in front of me, and wrote the rest of it myself.

I remember an older girl called Janet coming to play with us. One day she brought a little cushion with an opening at one corner. Inside there were scraps of beautiful fabrics. She let us take them out one at a time and look at them. It was wonderful.

I remember playing a record of 'Lillibulero' and dancing round and round the wind-up gramophone.

I remember dreaming that I could fly. I didn't go high up but I could lift my feet off the ground and move effortlessly through the air. I still have this dream sometimes.

I remember dreaming that someone was tickling me and wouldn't stop and it was really horrible, so I bit them as hard as I could. I still have this dream too.

I remember when our South African aunt and cousins came to see us. I had been expecting black people in grass skirts and I was disappointed.

I remember finishing the last of Enid Blyton's *Malory Towers* books and wishing there were more.

I remember Nanna keeping us out of the way because Daddy needed to talk with Mummy about the business.

I remember saying goodbye to my parents at Charing Cross station when I was seven and first went to boarding school. I didn't cry because the girls in books didn't cry.

I remember the first time I saw a slug. It was a big black one, moving up the wall of the school dining room. I couldn't take my eyes off it because it was so horrible. I thought to myself: 'That must be a slug.'

I remember the first time I ate baked beans. We had them at school, on fried bread, and I liked them a lot. I still do.

I remember the matron putting a kaolin poultice on my knee after a girl pushed me over on the Sunday afternoon walk.

I remember permanganate of potash. It made the water bright purple and you had to sit with your feet in it.

I remember stone hot-water bottles.

I remember being part of a gang called The EE (it stood for Eating Eight). We stole spring onions from the kitchen garden.

I remember wishing I could run fast and be good at games.

I remember my best friend coming out of the cloak-room on a cold day, wearing a big coat with a hood, and saying, 'I'm an Omo.' She often got things wrong in ways that were funny and that was one of the reasons I liked her so much.

I remember a girl called Helen, who bossed us around.

I remember learning to sing 'The Ashgrove' and 'Linden Lea' and 'Early One Morning'.

I remember conducting the percussion band on Open Day. The teacher chose her favourite, Gina, but it turned out Gina couldn't beat 4/4 time. I was the only one who could.

I remember feeling sorry for a girl called Jane because I thought she was very ugly. When Mick Jagger became famous, it struck me that he looked just like Jane.

I remember reading under the bedclothes and the torch-light getting dimmer and dimmer.

I remember wearing long grey socks, held up by garters.

I remember nametapes on everything.

I remember reading Kipling's *Jungle Books* and thinking they were the best books I'd ever read and feeling sad about saying goodbye to Baloo and Bagheera and their world.

I remember writing stories in an exercise book and telling people I wanted to be a writer.

I remember thinking poetry was mostly rather boring.

I remember picking up one of the Pooh books and realising for the first time that it was very funny. I reread both the books, laughing all the time.

I remember going with my sister to buy *Beano* and *Dandy* and sitting on a wall to read them because we weren't allowed them at home.

I remember my father reciting 'The Charge of the Light Brigade'. That was better than the poems we did at school.

I remember a Christmas tree that rotated and played a tune.

I remember those big old Christmas tree lights. When one bulb went, the whole lot stopped working. Grown-ups got very tetchy trying to find out which bulb needed replacing.

I remember watching the Coronation on television. Richard Dimbleby kept going on about how heavy the crown was and I cried.

I remember having a bilious attack, kneeling with my head over the toilet and feeling so ill I wished I could die.

I remember having chickenpox at school in a dormitory full of girls with chickenpox. We had a competition to see who could drink the most cups of tea in a day.

I remember dressing up in my party dress and standing in front of the mirror imagining I was a ballet dancer.

I remember daydreams about being a concert pianist.

I remember longing to have an older brother. My father was a widower when he married my mother. I used to fantasise that a half-brother would turn up out of the blue.

I remember being afraid that Daddy would die.

I remember pretending to think I was adopted and getting a lot of concerned attention and reassurance from my parents. I had been hoping to learn that I *was* adopted because it would make me more interesting.

I remember being told, repeatedly, that I was lucky to have curly hair.

I remember hating my hair and wishing it was straight.

I remember sulking because I was made to wear a hat to church in the school holidays.

I remember telling my mother that I hated her, and meaning it.

I remember choosing a book about natural history and being disappointed because it was about nature not about history.

I remember Nanna, a teetotaller, saying, 'I've never touched an alcoholic in me life.'

I remember using Daddy's oil paints to paint a picture of our garden. It was no good.

I remember our art teacher in the senior school, with her smock and her CND badge. She was only interested in the girls who were good at art.

I remember Miss Cox playing us a record of Mozart's *Eine Kleine Nachtmusik* in a class music lesson, and thinking to myself, 'I like this. I *really* like this.' And feeling pleased with myself for liking classical music.

I remember falling (briefly) in love with Cliff Richard when I was fourteen and we went to see him at the Palladium.

I remember falling in love with Frankie Vaughan and later with Anthony Newley, and writing a poem about the latter.

I remember falling in love with various older girls at school. Mostly they were the ones who sang solos in the choir.

I remember learning how to inhale cigarette smoke and feeling dizzy and having to lie down.

I remember an incident in a war story when an American airman touched a nurse's breasts. After that I began to have sexual fantasies.

I remember writing a poem about Princess Margaret's wedding.

I remember being ashamed of myself because I was overweight.

I remember being taken to see a doctor and told that I was losing weight too quickly.

I remember being glad that I was at boarding school because there were no boys there and I didn't have to worry about looking attractive.

I remember reading Keats and thinking I would like to marry a poet and be his soulmate. I had forgotten all about wanting to be a writer myself.

Areté 2005

The Dogs

Husky was some kind of terrier – white/grey. The other day someone was talking about Sealyhams and that rang a bell. I think Husky was a Sealyham. And I think I remember him but I'm not sure. I have a photo of him with me, as a toddler, standing beside him. My parents told me that I called him 'Hucky-boy'. When he heard a motorbike on the road he would charge excitedly down the garden. If I was in the way, tough luck. I would stagger into the house saying, 'Hucky-boy knock me over.'

My father told us about the dog he had while he was married to his first wife. When she died, it was just him and the dog. Then the dog died. He was so devastated that he vowed he would never become attached to another dog. This resolve lasted until he got Husky, which must have been soon after I was born, if not before. His first wife, Edie, died in 1940. Four years later he married my mother. So he was dogless for five or six years at most.

He did get fond of dogs. I'm not sure, now, what kind of person my father was. For a long time I idealised him and now I'm not sure what kind of person he was. But he did get fond of dogs.

I don't remember the end of Husky – how or why he disappeared from our lives.

The next dog was Sandy, the corgi. The corgi who bit people. Or perhaps it was just one person: Mrs Filmer, a neighbour, who used to come in to use our telephone. She wore glasses. For some reason Sandy used to jump up and try to attack her glasses. One day he bit her, possibly on the face. Did he bite anyone else? I'm not sure. In any case, he had to go. He was taken in by Mrs Cantello, the fashion buyer at Mitchells. Mitchells of Erith was a department store and Daddy was the chairman and managing director. Mrs Cantello didn't have any children. This was mentioned as an explanation of the fact that she could manage Sandy and we couldn't. Since Sandy's problem, if I remember rightly, was with grown-up visitors, the explanation doesn't make much sense.

I believe I had a vague feeling, even then, that Sandy's behaviour had something to do with the way he was treated at our house – the angry anxiety about keeping him under control. I didn't know the word neurotic in those days. But I suspected that Mrs Cantello would be wiser and kinder than my parents in her dealings with him.

There was a gap, I don't know how long. We tried again. The next dog was Lassie, a mongrel, who looked as if she had a lot of spaniel in her. Black and white. She arrived as a tiny, sweet little puppy, and she grew and grew. We found ourselves with an unexpectedly large dog. My mother was always against the idea of a big dog: 'They cost so much to feed.' Lassie was uncontrollable. She used to charge around the house and garden, barking and knocking things over. She didn't obey orders. She upset my mother a lot. For a time Lassie lived in a kind of pen outside the back door, made out of sections of wire fencing. At first the fencing wasn't high enough and she jumped over it. Inside her pen she would rush around and bark her head off. My sister and I felt sorry for her.

There was bad feeling between us and the older generation over Lassie. I suppose we identified with her. We had arguments with our parents, in which we defended the dog. I had a feeling that Lassie's 'hysterical' behaviour (the word 'hysterical' was used of her and also, sometimes, of us) was in some way the result of the way she was treated – that she was a fellow victim of our mother's controlling personality.

And what of our father, who got fond of dogs? He may have felt some sympathy for Lassie. But mostly he just seemed fed up with her. She caused problems for Mummy, and that was a problem for Daddy. She was a worse nuisance than Sandy.

Eventually Lassie went to live with Mrs Arnold. She was our 'daily help', paid to clean the house. When we were small she was there (I think) five mornings a week. I loved her. I went on loving her until she died at the age of ninety and I still love her.

Mrs Arnold was fond of Lassie. She never uttered a word of criticism of my parents for the way they treated the dog or their children. She was kind to Lassie, and when my parents couldn't stand the dog any longer, Mrs Arnold took her home. I can't remember what we heard about Lassie after that, or how long she lived.

I sometimes wished Mrs Arnold could take us home, too, and love us and look after us. I don't think she would have minded. She had two grandsons about the same age as us – Peter and Gerald. We heard a lot about them. She had several sons. Later I learned that she had had one daughter, who died as a child. I saw a picture. She looked a bit like me.

The last of the dogs was Chippy, short for Chipolata, a dachshund. Black with some brown underneath. There was another gap, of course, between Lassie and Chippy. It surprises me, now I come to think about it, that my mother was willing to countenance the idea of another dog.

Chippy spanned the end of my childhood. We got him while we were still living in Barnehurst and I was still at school – in the late 1950s, probably. He moved with us to Bexhill in September 1963. By then I had left school, spent two months in a language school in Germany, and was waiting to go up to Oxford in October. It was quite a dramatic rupture with the past, my parents moving to a new area at the same time that I went away to university.

Chippy worked out better than Sandy or Lassie. He was affectionate and reasonably well behaved. It looked as if my family had finally succeeded in bringing up a normal dog. There was one unusual thing about him, however: he hated going for walks. If you rattled his lead and said 'Walkies!' he hid under the settee. If I insisted on taking him out, he sat down on the pavement and wouldn't budge. In his dislike of organised exercise, Chippy reminded me of myself. He did get some exercise, though, running round the garden. He was a small dog, and perhaps that was enough.

After leaving Barnehurst, Chippy lived in two houses in Bexhill-on-Sea. The first was in South Cliff Avenue, very near the beach. The second (a bit cheaper and smaller because my mother was always agitating to move somewhere cheaper and smaller) was in a road beginning with W – Withyam Road, that's it. Further from the sea, miles from a bus stop, so Nanna, my mother's mother, who lived with us, couldn't take herself into town – or anywhere. My father had given up driving by this time but he never got on a bus, in any case. He was over eighty, had little desire to go anywhere, and was content to be driven by my mother.

Withyam Road was Chippy's last home and my father's last home, too. Sometime in 1970 the vet was called and he said the time had come to put Chippy out of his misery. He'd had a dodgy heart for a while. The vet said, 'Go and say goodbye to your master.' Chippy waddled into the lounge, where Daddy was sitting. Daddy cried. I wasn't there – my mother told me about it.

Poor old Chippy. I used to wonder how he felt. Was he happy? Was he bored? He was loved – by me and my sister, by my father, and probably by Nanna and my mother too. I think we managed, in spite of everything, to give at least one dog a reasonably good life.

Unpublished memoir

My Father

Daddy was a reader, who usually had a book on the go. He was particularly fond of Dickens. One of my regrets is that I didn't read much Dickens in his lifetime. I'd love to discuss it with him now. But most of his reading was non-fiction. He enjoyed military history. If a general published his memoirs, he solved somebody's problem about what to buy Daddy for Christmas. Judges' memoirs went down well too. There were several volumes on our bookshelves about famous court cases.

He had made a rule for himself that could not be broken. 'If I begin a book, I finish it.' This didn't only apply to single-volume works. Once he had embarked on Churchill's *History of the Second World War*, he went straight through it, without reading another book until he had reached the end. The Churchill wasn't a problem but he ran into trouble when he started reading a three-volume history of the migration of Persian tribes.

'Oh dear,' he would complain. 'This book is very boring.'

'Don't read it then!'

'Once I've started a book,' he would reply firmly, 'I finish it.' I can't remember how long the Persian tribes took him.

I'm surprised he didn't read more funny books. He had a good sense of humour. I imagine he might have appreciated P.G. Wodehouse but he probably regarded Wodehouse as a traitor. There were comedians whose work he enjoyed: Tommy Cooper, Harry Worth. He liked watching conjurors, such as David Nixon.

On the whole, though, he wasn't keen on television. If the rest of us were watching something, he would stay in the room and make comments: 'Oh dear, another murder!' or 'Funny how the cowboys ride around with gramophones on the backs of their horses.'

During quiz shows he sometimes pretended to be asleep until he knew one of the answers. Then he'd sit up and bark '"Burial of Sir John Moore after Corunna!"' or '"Lays of Ancient Rome!"'

He liked watching cricket. If there was a Test Match, and he wasn't working, he would watch it all day. In the holidays I watched with him and got quite keen on the game. I knew all about Len Hutton, Peter May, Colin Cowdrey, Fred Trueman and Denis Compton.

When I was ten I was referred to an orthopaedic surgeon called Mr Tucker because of my flat feet and knock knees and hopelessness at sport. He told my parents I would never be an athlete, which was no surprise to any of us.

When we came out, Denis Compton was in the waiting room. Years afterwards Daddy would say to me, 'Do you remember how excited you were when we saw Denis Compton in Mr Tucker's waiting room?'

'Yes,' I always replied. And it was true. But I wasn't nearly as excited as Daddy. It made his day. Accompanying a child to a medical appointment isn't a fun day out but he must have been glad he came along on that occasion.

Daddy's presence at that appointment turned out to be very fortunate for me too. Mr Tucker recommended night splints to remedy my knock knees. I knew about night splints because my friend Rosemary already had them. Every night the matron came into our dormitory and bandaged them onto her legs. I felt sorry for her. When Mr Tucker said I had to have them, my heart sank.

But I was spared. It seemed miraculous at the time. Daddy announced that he didn't think it was worth making me miserable, just to cure my knock knees. I expected my mother to try and overrule him but she went along with it. I never had to be bandaged into splints. Have I still got knock knees? I neither know nor care.

Daddy was born in 1885, and christened Fred Stanley. Not Frederick: Fred. By the time I knew him his hair was grey, he was bald on top and he had a bit of a stomach. Photographs show that he had been a good-looking young man. As an older man, he still had a handsome face.

He left school at the age of fourteen and became an apprentice draughtsman at Fraser and Chalmers in Erith, an electrical engineering firm. After his time there, the firm became part of GEC.

He began working for them in 1899, the year that saw the start of the Boer War. He told us that he volunteered to join the army and serve in South Africa. He was too young to serve overseas (the minimum age was sixteen, I think – possibly seventeen) but he lied about his age and got some way with the application procedure before he was found out. They wouldn't let him join up.

In 1914 he again wanted to volunteer but he wasn't allowed to because his job was designated a 'reserved occupation'. This was the era when patriotic ladies went round giving out white feathers to men of fighting age who weren't in uniform. In her *Testament of Youth*, Vera Brittain describes what a difficult time her uncle had. He couldn't join up because he worked for the Bank of England. Daddy was dead by the time I realised what he might have gone through at this time. Perhaps it is as well. If he did have to put up with being treated as unpatriotic and a coward, it evidently wasn't something he wanted to talk to us about.

By 1939 he was too old to join the regular services and had to content himself with the Home Guard. I have a silver cigarette box inscribed: 'To Major F.S. Cope with best wishes from his brother officers of the 56th Kent Bn Home Guard. January 1944.' That was the month he married my mother, so perhaps it was a wedding present. He was subsequently promoted to lieutenant colonel but the war ended before the promotion was announced in the *London Gazette*, so it never became official.

It was clear from the way he talked about the Home Guard that he had enjoyed it and that he was proud of his service. When the Home Guard became a joke, with the advent of the television programme *Dad's Army*, I think he was hurt.

He always said that he would have liked to be a lawyer or a soldier. Economic circumstances were a bar to the former ambition but I'm not sure what stopped him joining up as a regular soldier in peacetime, when he was old enough. I can speculate. As a young man he was 'genteel poor', with the accent and demeanour of a middle-class person. He was a fairly quiet and shy person, not the type to go to the pub and laugh at dirty jokes. He didn't have the necessary educational background or financial resources to train as an officer. It is hard to imagine him fitting in as a private soldier.

Whatever the reason, he continued to work as a draughtsman until he met Hedley Mitchell. I believe they served together in the Territorial Army between the wars. Hedley Mitchell was the founder and owner of a department store, Mitchells of Erith (regrettably there was no apostrophe). Hedley offered my father a job, which he took. Some time before the outbreak of the Second World War, the boss, who was in poor health, went to South Africa, with his South African wife and his children, and left my father in charge of the business.

Hedley died during the war. Thereafter my father ran the business as an employee of the Mitchell family. The widow, Cissie Mitchell, was my godmother. She lived in a big house called Atherfolds, at Ide Hill in Kent.

When I was five years old my parents went on a P&O cruise, leaving us with Nanna. My father was taken ill and the ship's doctors couldn't figure out what was wrong with him. When they got back, he was driven straight to Guy's Hospital. My mother arrived home in an understandably grim and anxious mood. While Daddy was in hospital, Aunty Cissie offered to have me to stay. This was a golden interlude in my childhood. Atherfolds was surrounded by farmland. I think she owned the farm and employed a manager. It was like being sent to stay in a children's book. Cows. Sheep. Barns. Fields. Farmyard smells. We'd visited Aunty Cissie for lunch or tea often enough, but I'd never had the chance to wander round the farm. The youngest Mitchell child, John, who was five or six years older than me, showed me round and introduced me to the farm workers and the animals. The two older children, Margaret and Ellen, then in their teens, looked after me and read me stories at bedtime.

One day, while we were eating lunch (it was probably called lunch at Atherfolds), Aunty Cissie jumped up with a cry of dismay. The cows had invaded her garden and were munching the flowers. We all went and yelled at them and shooed them out. This incident proved memorable because it seemed *just* the kind of thing that might happen in an Enid Blyton story.

Daddy recovered. He told it this way. The doctors were very concerned because he wasn't eating. One of them said to him, 'Is there anything at all that you fancy eating?'

'Yes,' said my father. 'I think I could manage some roast pheasant.'

They arranged for roast pheasant to be brought to his room and he ate it. That was the beginning of his recovery. Roast pheasant on the National Health Service? No. He was in the private wing.

They never did find out what was wrong with him. It was presumed to be some obscure tropical bug. After the dreadful night when they first got back from the cruise, I don't remember worrying about him. I was too busy having fun at Atherfolds. Afterwards, though, I understood that Daddy had been close to death and this must have increased my sense of his vulnerability.

Although Aunty Cissie was good to me, my sister and I couldn't help noticing that she looked like a turkey. She had a lot of loose skin on her long neck, and, if I remember rightly, her face was often red. She was a strong personality and she could upset people.

My parents were careful about what they said in front of us but I sensed that she wasn't their favourite person. Eventually they fell out with her.

In the late 1950s and early 1960s the business wasn't doing well. It was difficult for independent department stores to compete with chains. Many were taken over, but I don't know of any offers for Mitchells. Erith had a problematic catchment area, with the River Thames on one side, so there were no customers from that direction. Nearby Bexleyheath was developing into a popular shopping centre. The shop needed modernising but the capital wasn't available.

There were meetings with consultants and accountants. First they closed the branches – four shops called Mother and Baby, in Ashford, Sevenoaks, Tonbridge and West Wickham. Then it was decided that Mitchells itself would have to close.

My father had no share in the business. There were negotiations about his severance deal and his pension. And my mother's too because she worked in the business. My parents felt that Aunty Cissie behaved badly towards them. If the consultants and accountants hadn't stuck up for them, they would have got an even worse deal.

I was fourteen or fifteen years old at the time, and I only know what they told me. Once Mitchells had closed, they lost touch with the Mitchell family. It didn't occur to me to try and keep in touch with my godmother. My parents wouldn't have liked it, and I was at an age when one isn't good about bothering with aunties.

By the time the shop closed and he retired, Daddy was seventy-five, too old and tired to want to travel or find new hobbies. At one time he had enjoyed oil painting. My mother encouraged him to take this up again but it didn't last long. They moved to Bexhill-on-Sea, a town populated largely by pensioners. It wasn't a good idea. In Erith my father had been somebody; in Bexhill he was just a likeable old man. He sat in his armchair, smoked his pipe and read books and newspapers. At the age of eighty-five, he fell over and broke a leg. He went into hospital, where he died of pneumonia in January 1971.

Unpublished memoir

My Mother's Story

My relationship with my mother was not a happy one. I have touched on this in some of my poems and in one or two pieces in this book. My attempts to write about it at greater length have helped me understand the problem but they haven't resulted in anything I want to publish. What follows is an outline of the story of her life, leaving out most of the stuff that would turn it into a misery memoir.

My mother had a horrible childhood. She was born in 1916 to Eliza Lily and Thomas Hand. Eliza Lily (Nanna) grew up in or near Erith in Kent, where my mother was born. Thomas grew up in Hartlepool. I don't know when or why he came south, or how the couple met.

Their baby was christened Alice Mary but she wasn't called Alice for long. Thomas had a domineering sister called Elsie, who felt that her niece should be named after her. Somehow she managed to manipulate my grandparents into calling their daughter Elsie. Officially she remained Alice Mary but for most of her life she was known as Elsie.

When Elsie was two or three years old, her father fell

ill with tuberculosis. Nanna told me he caught it from a colleague at the factory where he worked. The colleague, according to Nanna, was careless about where he spat.

Thomas was ill for several years and died when my mother was nine. That must have been in 1925, when Nanna was twenty-nine or thirty. My mother was made to go to the funeral. She always said that she shouldn't have been made to go, that it was a terrible experience for a small child. I never dared to ask questions about that funeral. I wish, now, that I had. I want to understand the emotional damage my mother suffered, and the story of the funeral – how she felt and how she behaved – might tell me a lot.

Nanna once said to me that if she'd known how hard her life was going to be after the death of her husband, she wouldn't have been able to face it. They were very poor. Nanna worked in a baker's shop. When she was old and senile and couldn't remember what you said five minutes ago, she could still talk coherently about the shop – the cake-frills and decorations, the special orders. It wasn't a terrible job and her employers were kind to her. But she didn't earn much.

Many young women in Nanna's position would have turned to their parents for help. But Nanna's mother, by all accounts, was a monster. As a little girl, Nanna had measles and temporarily lost her eyesight. While she was blind, her mother punished her for knocking things over. When Nanna got married her family disapproved because they were Conservative and Thomas was a Liberal. They also disliked the fact that he was a devout Baptist. They were not keen on religion.

Elsie's lifelong Christian faith may have sprung from loyalty to her lost and idealised father. As a teenager she left the Baptist Church and joined the Church of England. She said she changed her mind about infant baptism (Baptists believe that people shouldn't be baptised until they are adults). She also admitted that she wanted to go to a different church from her mother. But she was always a very low Anglican, with little interest in the history or traditions of the Church, and little sympathy with the broad, tolerant outlook of middle-of-the-road Anglicans. Once, over lunch, my father said he thought that perhaps all religions were worshipping the same God in their different ways. My mother responded sharply, 'Don't say things like that in front of the children.'

When Nanna was widowed and working full time, she had to find somewhere for her daughter to go at dinner-time. You couldn't have dinner at school. Nanna's mother agreed to give Elsie her dinner. As soon as the child finished eating, she was expected to leave. The dinner-break wasn't over, and she wasn't allowed back into school, so she hung around the school gates. When her teachers noticed this, they took pity on her and let her in early.

She loved her teachers. She kept in touch with one of them, Miss Loveday, and sometimes took my sister and me to see her. When Miss Loveday died, Elsie was one of a very small handful of mourners at the funeral.

My mother was clever at school – there are school prizes to prove it. When she was eleven she had the chance to go to the grammar school. You didn't have to pay fees but you did have to buy a uniform. Nanna said she couldn't afford it. My mother resented this for the rest of her life. She felt that Nanna could have found a way of affording it, somehow, if she had really wanted her to take advantage of the opportunity. It must have been unbearably frustrating for a bright, hard-working girl.

Elsie went to Erith Central School with the girls who were not grammar school material. She left at fourteen, took a job in an office and went to evening class to learn shorthand and typing. I'm not sure how many jobs she had before she went to work at Mitchells. I know one of them was with an insurance company. A Miss Hill, who had been a colleague there, sometimes visited when we were children.

Landing the job at Mitchells changed my mother's life. She was secretary to the chairman and managing director – Mr Fred S. Cope. His first wife was still alive when Elsie began working for him. It must have been in the late 1930s.

After my father was widowed (in about 1940) there was more than one woman after him. At least one of the hopefuls (other than my mother) was an employee. When his engagement to the young Miss Elsie Hand was announced, there was some bad feeling and nastiness. My parents sometimes talked about this, laughing at the spinster and the widow who had set their caps at Daddy. If these people were nasty to them, I suppose it was fair enough to poke fun at them years afterwards. As a child I enjoyed the stories and joined in the laughter. As an adult, I have some sympathy with the spinster and the widow.

I was rather proud of the age gap between my parents. It made our family different and special and got me attention when I told anyone. I liked explaining how I got my name. When my father asked my mother to marry him he said, 'Of course, I'm very old.'

'No,' she responded. 'You're like Peter Pan. You don't grow old.' They began calling each other Peter and Wendy. When my mother was pregnant with me they saw a boat at Hastings called *Wendy Mary* and decided that would be the baby's name. They were certain I was a girl.

Everyone called me Wendy Mary for the first seven years of my life. When I went to boarding school I feared it was the kind of name that might cause me trouble. I hadn't yet come across Violet Elizabeth Bott but I had noticed that the popular girls in books tended not to have two Christian names. With an assertiveness that surprises me, looking back, I decided to tell people at school that I was called Wendy. That was simple. When I went home at the end of term I announced that I was Wendy now and got away with it. That surprises me too. From then on my parents called each other Fred and Elsie. Was that sad for them? I sometimes used to feel guilty about it but it has recently occurred to me that dropping the twee nicknames may have been a relief.

The young wife developed into a capable business-woman. My father relied greatly on her help in running the firm. And she was active in the locality, serving at different times as President of Inner Wheel, Chairman of Erith Chamber of Commerce, and Chair of the local Guides. Nanna lived with us and did much of the child-care and domestic work.

These were, I believe, the best years of my mother's life. Once or twice she met another young wife married to an older man: Margaret Thatcher, the Conservative candidate for the Dartford constituency. Although her politics were Conservative, she always said she hadn't liked Mrs Thatcher. I suspect this was largely due to envy. The politician was a bit younger, a bit more glamorous, much better educated, and likely to succeed in a bigger pond than the one Elsie was swimming in. None the less, Elsie was having a pretty nice life in the Erith pond.

Once my father retired, the good times were over. My mother was still in her forties when she settled in Bexhill with an old and increasingly sedentary husband. She was active in the local church and in Inner Wheel and did voluntary work. She made friends. She took me on a holiday to Italy because my father didn't want to go. He spent the whole fortnight in a state of utter misery and anxiety. When we got back he made my mother promise never to go away for so long again. She did occasionally absent herself for a few days to visit her cousin Evelyn in Wales. She rang home every evening at six o'clock. According to Nanna, he would go and sit by the phone soon after 5.30 to wait for her call.

After my father's death, Evelyn and her husband persuaded my mother to go and live near them, in a small village outside Wrexham. She planned to spend the rest of her life there but a surprise lay in store. Over the years our family had become friendly with that of my school friend Rosemary. Her mother died of cancer the same week that my father succumbed to old age.

Four years after these two deaths, Rosemary's father, Val, asked my mother to marry him and she accepted. She moved back south to live with him and they were together for more than twenty-five years until his death in 2003. She survived him by eighteen months. Like my father, she died a few weeks after falling and breaking a leg. She was eighty-seven.

Nanna moved with my mother to Wales and then back south to the new marital home. In 1982, at the age of eighty-five, she fell over, broke an arm, and died of a heart attack the next day. Since I've been a senior citizen, one or two people have commented on my apparently neurotic fear of falling over.

Unpublished memoir

Mitchells

Mitchells of Erith. I remember dark, shiny, heavy counters and display units. I remember pots of cash whizzing around the store on overhead wires. On Saturdays Nanna worked on the cash desk, emptying these containers and sending them off again, with fresh supplies of small change. If I was in the shop, I'd go and say hello to her, and I could tell she was enjoying herself.

Apart from food and drink, the shop sold just about everything a person might need: clothes, cosmetics, china and glass, electrical goods, haberdashery, dress material, furniture and carpets. The last of these was my favourite department. As a small child I loved looking at the beautiful patterns on the oriental rugs. Although you couldn't buy groceries, you could get coffee or lunch in the Oak Room, a restaurant named after its dark, heavy tables and chairs. The Oak Room opened in the late 1950s, a few years before dark, heavy furniture went right out of fashion.

My father's office was on the first floor, up a flight of stairs near the electrical and carpet departments. If I went and said hello to him, I was allowed to have a go on his swivelling chair. On the wall behind his desk there was a framed motto: 'Punctuality is the soul of business, and the acid test of personal efficiency.' There was no author's name on this pearl of wisdom. I assumed it was F.S. Cope but, regrettably, I never checked the assumption.

There were two desks in the office. The other one was sometimes used by my mother, who by then was company secretary, and sometimes by my father's secretary, Miss Hart. Miss Hand, who gave her hand in marriage to her boss, was succeeded by Miss Hart. Fortunately Miss Hart did not give her heart to the boss but to a rather good-looking young husband, whose name I have forgotten.

Daddy seemed to like it when I visited him in the office and always made me feel welcome. If there were times when I had to go away because he was busy, I can't remember them. It occurs to me that I got a friendlier reception when he was at work than when he was at home.

Everyone in the shop was nice to me and to my sister. Yes, we were the boss's daughters and they couldn't very well not be. But I think that, even as a child, I could tell the difference between genuine warmth and polite pretence. And I believe there was genuine warmth towards us, especially from those members of staff who had been around for a while. They had known my father as a childless widower in his fifties and there had been (or so I was told) great excitement about his getting married again, and then becoming a father at the age of fifty-nine.

My parents used to say that the person who had been most thrilled by the news was Miss Tucker, a happily married woman with a daughter who would have been a teenager at the time. She was the buyer for perfumery and haberdashery. Her husband, Mr Cartwright, was the buyer for menswear. They met through work and, after they were married, she continued to be known by her maiden name. Mr Cartwright always had a twinkle in his eye when he addressed her as Miss Tucker. That was what we called them when we were small but at some point it was agreed that in future they would be Aunty Bob and Uncle Maurice.

I loved them both. Aunty Bob had dark hair, which stayed dark so long I think it must have been dyed. She was a fat lady, but an attractive one, always well dressed and made up. I remember her as a warm, smiling person, who always made me feel that it was a treat to see me. Uncle Maurice, too, was warm and kind, and something of a comedian. He had some party pieces – 'Albert and the Lion' was one of them – that we loved to hear him recite. He was good-looking and always beautifully dressed.

Uncle Maurice had seen action in the trenches during the First World War. He didn't talk about it, except to tell us that he had been at Ypres and that the soldiers all called the place Wipers. He taught my sister to play pontoon. My mother was a bit iffy about this, because pontoon is a gambling game, but fondness for Uncle Maurice won out over her puritan streak and she settled for amused tolerance.

I don't know how many years the Cartwrights worked in the shop. They had been there since long before I was born. At some point during my childhood my parents came home and announced that Uncle Maurice had been made a director of the company. Another member of staff who became a director was Victor Hodges. He was a pale, thin young man who didn't impress me much at first, though I came to respect and like him. He married Miss Rosina White, who worked in china and glass. After Mitchells closed he went on to have a successful career in a chain of department stores.

Mitchells of Erith, department store and marriage bureau. Mr Hollifield, buyer of electrical goods was married to a colleague who was still known at work as Miss Boshier. Jill Brett, who worked for a while as our nanny, later moved to a job in the shop and married a young man she met there. Alongside these happy romances there must have been some unhappy ones – break-ups, heartbreak and infidelity – but the boss's daughters didn't get to hear about such things.

One little bit of excitement in our lives was that Mrs Hancock, who ran the theatre ticket bureau, had a daughter, Sheila, who was just beginning to get work as an actress. When she appeared as Dick Whittington at Bromley Rep we were taken along. Afterwards we went backstage to see Sheila and be introduced to the pantomime cat. Sometimes Sheila, tall, blonde and glamorous, came into the shop to see her mother. In her memoir, *Ramblings of an Actress*, she recalls 'comfortable ladies and neat gentlemen . . . taking pride in counter displays of gloves, hankies, discreet undies, artificial flowers and hats, and the neatly stacked rolls of material which they ripped flamboyantly into the length required'. She, too, was 'spellbound' by the 'magic contraption which flew off on wires to the cash desk'. 'It was', she concludes, 'a lovely place.'

I am grateful for that observation. I, too, had the impression that Mitchells was a happy place to work, and that my father had a good relationship with the staff. But I was only fourteen when the business closed down, and I mostly heard management's side of the story. From Sheila's perspective it might have looked very different, and I am glad that it did not.

Who else do I remember? Mrs Cantello, the fashion buyer, has already been mentioned as the person who took over one of our dogs. She was a tall, slim, smart lady, who often did me a favour by telling my mother, 'I've got something that would just suit Wendy.' She ended a long-running dispute between my mother and me about winter coats. Having paid a hefty price for my school uniform coat, my mother thought I could jolly well wear it in the holidays as well. It was a horrible coat, made of scratchy ginger tweed. One day Mrs Cantello showed us a gorgeous geranium-red one and mentioned that it might look nice on me.

'Can I try it on?' I asked.

'All right,' said my mother, in a voice that suggested she knew the battle was lost.

It did suit me and she bought it. I hope the hugs and gratitude and my evident pleasure in wearing it made her feel the money was well spent. In fact, she didn't have to pay as much as any ordinary customer. Everything we bought at Mitchells was cost price. No wonder my mother resented paying the full retail price to the suppliers of our uniform.

On one occasion my father came with me to the shoe

department. I picked out several pairs to try on. The first pair fitted. 'If those fit,' said Daddy, 'why try on the others?' That taught me that men have a different attitude to shopping and it isn't a good idea to take one with you.

As well as the departments in the shop, Mitchells had a fleet (probably a small fleet) of removal vans. There was a man called Bert Gibbs (Mr Gibbs to us), who was a driver, and who often turned up at our house. I'm not sure what he was doing there. I think my parents may have paid him to do odd jobs – or perhaps he was delivering stuff. Anyway, my father told us that Mr Gibbs had been a prisoner of the Japanese during the war. The Japanese were very cruel to their prisoners and he had had a terrible time and he didn't like to talk about it. He was a strong, healthy-looking man, still young when I knew him in the 1950s.

Then there was Mr Coles, who was old when I knew him. He worked for Mitchells as a carpenter. I remember him for two reasons. He had a houseboat on the Thames and once took us for a great day out on it. And he made me a christening present that I still treasure. It is a moneybox in the shape of a book. The cover is dark wood, and on the spine it says 'Wendy Mary 1945' in gold letters. Since I began earning my living as a writer, this gift has seemed wonderfully prescient.

Unpublished memoir

Billy Graham

I was nine years old in 1954 when I went to hear Billy Graham. My mother, a keen evangelical Christian, had decided to go and listen to a relay of his Harringay meeting in our local Baptist church. I've always thought it must have required considerable persuasion to get me to go with her but I was assured, in a conversation with her, that I didn't need persuading – I begged to be taken along.

I find this surprising. We were C of E. I believed in God and Jesus, Heaven and Hell, and regarded church as something boring that you had to put up with. However, if my mother's account is true, it seems that I volunteered for some extra religion on a weekday evening.

I can remember that the Baptist church was full and that there was some singing. Apart from that I have little recollection of what went on before Billy Graham spoke. I probably wasn't paying much attention.

The part I shall never forget was the climax of his talk, so eloquent and gripping that not even a dreamy nine-year-old could fail to take it in. He quoted that favourite text of evangelicals: 'I am the Way, the Truth and the Life. No man cometh unto the Father but by me.' He said a lot about faith and asked each one of us to accept the Lord Jesus Christ as our own *personal* Saviour. It wasn't enough just to do this in your heart – you had to get up and 'come forward'.

'If you can't come forward', he boomed, 'and stand before these people gathered here today and show that you have accepted the Lord Jesus Christ as your own personal Saviour, how will you ever stand before your Heavenly Father on the Day of Judgement?'

To make a spectacle of myself in front of all these people was the last thing I wanted. But the logic of his words seemed unanswerable: either I did this or I would burn in Hell for ever. The Heavenly Father was making an offer I couldn't refuse.

When Graham had finished speaking there was organ music while everyone prayed. I tapped my mother on the arm.

'I'm going up.'

'All right,' she whispered.

Knowing she was pleased didn't make it any better. I took a deep breath, got to my feet, and squeezed past the rest of our row.

At Harringay they went forward in hundreds. At Erith Baptist Church there was only me. For a few dreadful minutes I had to stand by myself at the front while they waited to see if anyone else would join me. Then the minister, a kind and good-looking man called Mr Brown, came and smiled at me and took me backstage to the church hall.

There I was introduced to a Mrs Johnson and told she was my counsellor. We went into a booth together and she talked to me for about twenty minutes, asking questions as she went along to make sure I understood.

I understood very well and felt intensely miserable. I was committing myself more deeply to a life of prayer, Bible-reading and church, and I didn't expect it to be any fun at all. What upset me even more was the invasion of my privacy, the feeling that part of my inner life was being put on show and taken over by other people. Although I disliked church, I did love Jesus – I always had – and I didn't want it to be anyone's business but mine.

Guiltily, I struggled to repress these feelings and to convince myself and Mrs Johnson that I was experiencing some kind of quiet holy joy. She seemed a nice lady. She gave me some Bible-study notes and a booklet of Bible quotations and, with a sad smile, said she would pray for me.

When we came out my mother and the minister were waiting for me. They looked happy.

'Well, Wendy,' said Mr Brown. 'Can you tell us what it is that you've done this evening?'

I knew what I was supposed to say but I couldn't bring myself to say it. I'd had enough. I wanted to burst into tears, run away, forget the whole thing. Instead I looked down at my shoes.

'I don't know,' I replied.

They went on smiling but I could see they were put out. It was a small protest but it was something.

We went home and my mother told my father what had happened. He believed in God but not, I now realised, in American evangelists. Without saying much, he made it clear that he wasn't overjoyed. Upstairs in bed, after trying to pray and read my Bible, I cried myself to sleep.

I am not now a churchgoer, nor have I ever been able to find the joy and peace in the Christian religion that is, I know, experienced by some of my relations and friends. Resentment at my 'conversion' by Billy Graham is not the only reason for this, but it certainly hasn't helped.

He will be back later this year with a huge and well-publicised 'Mission England'. I hope that the crowds who flock to his meetings will leave their children at home.

Unpublished 1989

After I moved to Winchester in 1994 I began going to services in the cathedral.

Education, Education

My schooling began with a year at a progressive nursery, followed by two years at a convent, then boarding school at the age of seven, and another boarding school from the age of twelve. After university I worked as a primary school teacher, first in West Ham and later in Southwark. I was full-time from 1967 until 1981, when I managed to get myself seconded to a job on Contact, *the ILEA's newspaper for teachers. That was quite a nice job, although somewhat pointless because we were fairly sure no one read anything except the job advertisements. I once wrote and published half a page of spoof reviews of invented children's books. Nobody noticed. In 1984 I returned to teaching part-time, until 1986 when my first book was published.*

Going to School

One day, when I was three or four years old, I asked when I would be going to school.

'Do you want to go to school?' my mother asked.

'Yes. When can I go?'

'Would you like to go to school today?'

'Yes!'

'All right then. I'll take you after dinner.'

It seemed too good to be true, and it was. If I'd been a little bit older I would have worked out that I couldn't go to a proper school today because today was a Sunday.

My mother took me to the church hall. To Sunday school. Almost as soon as she had left I realised that this wasn't proper school but a cheat. What did we do that Sunday? Was it the usual sitting in groups looking at Bible pictures and listening to a Bible story? Or was that first Sunday the occasion when we all had to watch a slide show about Rochester Cathedral? The slides were not in colour, and I couldn't have been less interested.

In any case, I did not like Sunday school. I was made to go again but I don't remember going very often. It probably wasn't worth the sulking and the fuss.

Not long afterwards I was allowed to go to nursery school but this wasn't a proper school either. It was, though I didn't know the word then, progressive. In the morning there were all sorts of activities going on in different rooms and you could choose. On the first day I was shown to a room where you painted pictures. Every day after that I went to the same room because I was too timid to try any of the others.

I had one friend there, Rosanne, the daughter of our GP and his wife. Rosanne and I had been brought together to play all our lives, and I suppose we liked each other. I don't think I got on with the rest of the children. One school report survives from those days. It says, 'Wendy Mary is reluctant to share her activities with others.'

I wasn't at the nursery for very long. The next school was the convent. My mother, who began life as a Baptist and became a very low Anglican, was extremely suspicious of Roman Catholics. But the alternative was to send me to a local state school, where I would mix with the wrong sort of children and pick up the wrong accent. She opted for exposing me to the wrong religion, even though Madam Pius, headmistress of the convent, was famous for converting whole families.

The convent was, most definitely, a proper school. We sat down in classrooms and learned things. My class teacher was Madam Bernadette. We sat in groups at tables and learned reading. At my table we chanted the sounds that letters made: 'Ker-a-ter CAT, der-o-ger DOG.' The teacher didn't know that I had already learned to read at home.

My mother asked what I was doing at school and I told her about 'Ker-a-ter CAT'.

'That's ridiculous. I'll tell Madam Bernadette you can read.'

'No. Please don't tell her.' I was afraid I'd get into trouble.

I couldn't stop her, of course. Next day I was moved to a different group at the other side of the classroom. You were allowed to choose a book and read it. Just as I had predicted, Madam Bernadette seemed rather cross.

As a Protestant I was supposed to be 'withdrawn' from RE lessons. If this actually happened, I wonder why I can remember sitting in a classroom listening to a nun talk about the Virgin Mary. I put my hand up.

'What's a virgin?'

'A virgin is a young woman who has never done anything wrong.'

'Nothing? Ever? Not even when she was a little girl?'

'No. Nothing at all.'

Astonishing. Some years afterwards I found out what 'virgin' really means. But I still didn't put two and two together about the Virgin birth. I was about seventeen when the penny finally dropped, one Christmas. Virgin birth! So that's what all the fuss was about.

On another occasion (when I was no longer in Madam Bernadette's class) our teacher, whose name I can't recall, told us about St Bernadette and her vision at Lourdes. When she finished, I put my hand up.

'What did the Virgin Mary say to St Bernadette?'

'We don't know.'

'What, nobody knows?'

'No. Nobody knows.'

'Will we find out when we die and go to heaven?'

'Perhaps you will.'

I wanted to hurry up and die, so my curiosity could be satisfied.

Not long ago I told someone this story. He asked me, 'Do you still want to know what she said?'

I thought about it, and said, no, I didn't really care any more. We both felt that was rather sad.

One day – it must have been in February 1952 – a nun came into our classroom, looking very solemn, and whispered something to our teacher.

'Children,' she announced. 'I am very sorry to have to tell you that the King has died.' She said the chapel would be open at dinner-time so people could go and pray for his soul.

The school chapel was very beautiful, or so it seemed to me. It was full of pictures and colours and shiny things – much better than the church my mother took me to. I was scared of going in on my own, so I found a Catholic girl in our class who was willing to come with me. She showed me what to do with the holy water at the door. We knelt down for a short time. I did feel a bit sad about the King.

By the time I left the convent, despite my official non-attendance at RE lessons, I knew the Hail Mary off by heart. I was fascinated by the rosary and decided I'd like to have one of my own. So I asked my mother, 'Please may I have a rosary?'

Can I remember her face, or am I imagining it? Anyway,

she said no, and it was clear she wasn't pleased. Not long afterwards I was taken away from the convent and sent to boarding school. No one has ever told me that these events were connected but I believe they may have been.

Unpublished memoir

Going Away

My parents had something to tell me. They were sending me away to boarding school. Because they had decided it was best for me.

My mother's explanation was that I would be better off away from old people – my father and my grandmother. Nanna was nice to us, and much more patient than either of our parents, so the part of the argument involving her cuts no ice at all. But my father did find it difficult having young children around. I was born less than a month before his sixtieth birthday. When my sister came along he was sixty-two. We often had to be shushed and kept out of his way, especially when he had just got home from work. The responsibility for keeping us quiet and out of the way was my mother's, although she got a lot of help from Nanna.

When they told me about boarding school, I got a strong feeling that Daddy wasn't happy about it. This could have been wishful thinking but I don't believe it was. My mother did the talking, and he seemed sad. Of course, since he didn't have to look after us, there were fewer advantages from his point of view.

A list arrived of all the things you had to have at

boarding school. A grey skirt and a red jumper. A navy gym tunic and white shirts and a school tie. A school scarf and woolly hat (grey with red stripes and a covered button on top). School socks. Sandals and lace-up shoes. A blazer. A winter coat (navy). White knickers. Navy-blue knickers. Vests or liberty bodices. Nightdresses or pyjamas and a dressing gown and slippers. Shorts and Aertex shirts. Gym shoes. A rug and an eiderdown.

There were shopping trips to buy all this stuff. It was packed in a trunk, with each item crossed off as it went in. (Whenever I go away from home, I still have a list and cross off each item.)

The day before I was due to leave I had a chat with Mrs Arnold. I admitted that I didn't really want to go. As we talked I was cuddling Roger, my teddy bear.

Mrs Arnold said, 'Tell you what. I'll give Roger a big kiss and a cuddle. You take him to school with you and whenever you cuddle Roger it will be like I'm there.' I liked this idea very much.

My parents decided it was best for me to go to school on the train, with other children, rather than be taken by car. I don't know how the trunk got to school. They had a shop in Ashford, where the school was, so perhaps it was delivered by van. My dark red 'weekend' case came with us to London – Charing Cross or Waterloo.

Sometime in the 1970s I wrote a poem, 'Going Away', about that day. This is the first stanza.

> *On the platform where the school train left,*
> *Seven years old, she didn't cry*

> *But smiled and chattered*
> *Like the schoolgirls she had met in books,*
> *Kissed her parents and went away.*
> *She never really came back.*

Almost as soon as I was on the train, someone said, 'You've got a watch. Look! She's got a watch!' Watches, I learned, were not allowed.

'I didn't know,' I said, trying not to cry. It was upsetting to discover I'd broken a rule already. When we got to school I found I had broken another one because I had a torch, and that wasn't allowed either. I didn't get told off but my watch and my torch – things my parents had given me to help with boarding-school life – were taken away.

This is the second stanza of 'Going Away':

> *The dormitory was dark. She longed*
> *For one slim triangle of moonlight*
> *Where the curtains didn't meet.*
> *It was as if black felt*
> *Were pressed against her face*
> *And it was hard to breathe.*

It turned out that homesickness was less uncommon in real life than in books. One or two girls cried in the dark, even though they weren't new, and the others were sympathetic. Somebody asked me if I was feeling homesick.

'Yes,' I replied. I cuddled Roger and thought about Mrs Arnold, and about how upset Mummy and Daddy would be if they knew my watch and torch were against the rules, and I cried too.

The first year dormitory, if I remember rightly, was called Pixies. In the second year you went into Elves. Then what? Possibly Fairies. There was one single room, for naughty or sick children. It was called the Squirrel's Nest.

In Pixies there were six of us, all aged seven to eight. We had iron bedsteads and a chair and a mat beside the bed. Bedtime, in the first year, was 6.45 p.m. In cold weather you were offered a hot-water bottle. Some of the school's bottles were the old stone kind. I must be one of the youngest people to have slept with one of these.

After lights out you weren't allowed to talk. This rule was enforced by our fierce matron. The matron must have been in her forties or fifties when I joined the school. She had short dark hair (not much grey, so perhaps forties, rather than fifties). She wore a white overall most of the time. When she was cross, she was frightening.

She didn't use physical violence. The punishment for persistent talking after lights out was to stand in a corridor for a while. This wasn't too bad, as long as she didn't forget you. If you were very bad, you had to go and sleep all night on a long white cupboard. Matron sometimes got cross with people who went to the toilet after lights out. She seemed to believe that we were doing it just for fun.

As well as Matron we had a young assistant matron. These tended not to stay long, so there were several in my time. The one I remember best is Jill Marshall. She was Miss Marshall to us, of course, but she didn't mind us knowing what her Christian name was. She had curly (or permed) hair and a curvaceous figure and she wore red lipstick. We thought her the epitome of glamour. And we liked her because she was kind to us. She listened to pop music on the radio. Thanks to Jill Marshall I know that 'Unchained Melody', played on the trumpet by Eddie Calvert, was a hit in the early 1950s. And that another of his hits was a number called 'Cherry Pink'. I can still sing both tunes. At home it wouldn't have occurred to anyone to listen to a station that played popular music.

As junior boarders we lived in Bridge House, across the road from the main school. Our housemistress was Miss Potter, who was OK. She was keen on Christianity and on games. In her daytime existence she was class teacher of the fourth years. In the house we didn't see all that much of her. But I was glad she was there, like God, as an ultimate authority less terrifying than the matron. After a couple of years Miss Potter left. Her replacement, Miss Jenkins, was also keen on Christianity and games. A small, dark woman with a nasty temper, she was a less benign figure than her predecessor.

School hours were a respite from life in Bridge House. We walked along a path for three or four hundred yards to Nightingale House, where our classrooms were.

In the classroom I had nothing to fear. The teachers were in charge and they were all reasonably humane. In the first year I had Miss Buckland – grey-haired and gentle. In the second year it was Mrs Dupont. She wasn't as nice as Miss Buckland. She seemed to fancy herself as rather sophisticated and she sometimes made sarcastic remarks. Although I didn't like her much, I wasn't scared of her.

In the course of these two years, it turned out I was brainy. This was an unlooked-for bonus. I would gladly have swapped it for being good at games, but it was better than nothing. I saw other children get anxious and upset about their work, and I was grateful that I didn't need to worry.

In Bridge House, however, I didn't feel safe, at least not for the first year or two. There was some bullying, although we didn't call it that. We called it 'teasing'.

From time to time it would be open season on a particular individual. The word went round, 'We're teasing X.' Just verbal nastiness – it didn't get physical. The person concerned was ostracised for a while, then it stopped. Or Miss Potter got to hear of it, called us together, and made a speech, saying it was disgraceful. That worked.

Did I join in? I don't believe I did. Neither did I have the courage to speak out against the bullying. It scared me. I felt I could easily become a victim of it. I thought of myself as a natural victim, the sort of person they would pick on. The odd thing is that, on the whole, they didn't.

There were incidents – most of us suffered a bit at sometime. At one point a few girls decided to pick on me because I used too many long words. I made an effort not to and it passed. A little while afterwards a new girl arrived called Carolyn. She had a large vocabulary too, and she used it. I was afraid for her. I warned her not to use long words. But, when other children started to get at her about it, she took no notice. She went right on talking the way she talked. Her persecutors soon got bored. I learned something about life from that episode, and something about myself.

After breakfast in Bridge House we had to gather in the playroom. Miss Potter said a prayer, made announcements and, if necessary, told us off. Then we were sent out, or let out, depending on your point of view, for a compulsory circuit of part of the grounds.

There was an asphalt playground outside the house and, beyond that, a garden area, divided into plots for us to cultivate (we mostly tried to grow things that were edible). We had to run up the side of the playground and the gardens, across the top, and back down the other side. Good runners were competitive about it – there was some pushing and shoving to get into a good position at the start. I didn't bother. I was such a slow runner that I was always one of the last to finish.

Being athletic was one of the most important ways of gaining status in Bridge House. What else counted? I don't think being pretty helped a lot and being rich certainly didn't. If you were thought 'posh', you could be victimised for it. The best way to achieve a position at the top of the pecking order was simply to have a domineering personality. In every dormitory there was a boss figure, who ruled the roost. If you didn't want your life to be made a misery, it was important to keep in with this person. I usually managed it. Much of the time I persuaded myself that I quite liked Helen or Ava or whoever. When I think of them now, I feel something close to hatred.

In adult life, when I meet a woman who reminds me of the dormitory bosses I can't help but detest her. When I see adult women sucking up to someone similar, just like we did at school, I want to spit.

What helped me to survive in this world of bullies and victims was my friendship with Rosemary. We were drawn to one another in the first year, and we remained firm friends until I changed schools at the age of twelve. Rosemary shared my dislike of games and she made me laugh. She wasn't a bully. We kept out of it. We were safer as a pair than as isolated individuals.

At weekends the boarders had to line up two by two in crocodiles and go for walks. We were divided into two groups – the A walk was for the older girls and the B walk for the little ones, with their shorter legs. Rosemary and I never graduated from the B walk, which suited us fine. The teachers put us at the back, with responsibility for making sure that no one got left behind and lost.

I like walking nowadays but it isn't much fun in a crocodile. I still have a scar on my knee because, on one walk, the girl behind me didn't think I was going fast enough, and pushed me over.

Once we got out of the town we were allowed to break ranks and wander more informally. We were usually allowed to stop and play for a while, so I did get some pleasure from the walks. Before I went away to school I had had very little experience of the countryside. We lived in a suburb and our family outings were usually to the sea.

One of the destinations on school walks was called the Warren. It was a large sloping field covered in bracken, with lots of rabbit holes. Another was the New Road. The New Road was the Ashford bypass, which was under construction at the time. We walked along part of the route, where the land had been cleared but the road not yet laid. It was very muddy. This walk also took us into some woods.

There was a wood near our house in Barnehurst, called Bursted Wood, but we weren't allowed in it. Bad men were said to lurk there. So the woods outside Ashford were the first I had the chance to play in. I'd read lots of stories with woods in them – it was great to be in a real one.

The school grounds were good to play in too. At Bridge House, as well as the playground and the garden area, we had two big fields. At the end of one of them was a slope, big enough to slide down in snowy weather. The school had a couple of toboggans. When it wasn't your turn for a toboggan, you could use a tin tray.

There were trees round the edges of the fields, where we could set up dens and camps. At one time Rosemary and I and Carolyn took over a corner where there were four trees, with a space in the middle just the right size to be our base. I can't remember what we did there but it still pleases me to know that we managed to claim that space for ourselves, and that nobody contested it.

Later on in the Bridge House years I belonged to a gang called The EE, which had a base at the far side of the further field. We didn't tell anyone outside the gang what EE stood for. Only members knew that we were The Eating Eight. Our aim was to get hold of extra food. We stole spring onions from the kitchen garden – my only experience of knowingly stealing anything. (I inserted the word 'knowingly' when I recalled that I have stolen stationery from employers. At the time I didn't think of this as theft.) I loved spring onions then, and I still do.

Since our base was two fields and a playground away from Bridge House, we couldn't always be bothered to go back there when we needed the toilet. We peed on the grass instead. After a while the grass around our base was a deeper, lusher shade of green than the rest of the field. This amused us greatly. No one outside The EE understood why any mention of 'very green grass' was so hilarious.

It would be an exaggeration to call Bridge House Dickensian but there were some things that parents certainly wouldn't accept nowadays. The bathwater, for example. In order to economise on hot water, we bathed two at a time. Then another two children got into the same water, then another two. The bathwater turned a very dark grey, almost black. We got used to this and thought nothing of it. A day girl called Margaret came to board for a few weeks because her parents had to go abroad. Margaret took one look at the almost black bathwater and refused to get in it. She said it was disgusting and full of germs. We thought she was a softie – typical day girl.

Then there was lumpy meat. Before dinner the word would go round, 'It's lumpy meat.' Bad news. It was a meat stew consisting largely of gristle. We were supposed to eat up everything on our plates, so we had to sit there trying to chew and swallow gristle. Sometimes we hid bits in our pockets. My sister swears she was sick over her lumpy meat on one occasion and the matron told her to eat it up. She didn't, of course, and I don't know what happened after that. I can't remember what happened to people who left some lumpy meat. I suppose we were allowed to get up and go in the end.

As the end of term approached I dreaded going home, and as the holidays drew to a close I dreaded going back to school. Either way the adjustment was painful. Home was warmer and more comfortable and you didn't have to go outside and run around. And I hated parting from my parents. They say that children find it harder to leave unhappy homes than happy ones. But I don't suppose many boarding-school pupils of seven or eight find it easy.

I left home six times a year – at the end of every holiday and half-term. Then there were the Saturdays when my parents came to take me out. In my first year I looked forward to these occasions. Everyone did. It was understood that going out with your parents was a great treat.

Usually we drove to the seaside. A couple of times we went to Lympne airport to look at the planes. In those days you could put your car on an aeroplane and fly it to France. We watched the nose of the plane open and saw the cars drive on. And we had a good view of take-offs and landings.

We always had a nice lunch and a nice tea. It should

have been fun but I felt sad the whole time because we would have to say goodbye at the end of the day. Sometimes my mother had a migraine but made the effort to come anyway. This cast a pall over the day. I wished she would stay home when she was ill and let Daddy come on his own.

After a while I admitted to myself that my parents' visits upset me. But I knew there would be a frightful scene if I asked them not to bother. And, by the time I'd been at the school for two years, my sister had turned seven and joined me there, so they weren't just coming to see me.

Unpublished memoir

Daddy Played 'Chopsticks'

I don't know how my mother acquired her interest in classical music. It certainly wasn't from my grandmother, who lived with us when I was a child and didn't die until I was nearly forty. I don't remember her ever listening to music. My maternal grandfather died of TB when my mother was nine years old. No one ever mentioned that he was keen on music of any kind. She must have discovered music at school, at church, and through friends.

My grandfather worked in a factory. After he died life was a struggle for his widow and daughter. I'm pretty sure they didn't have a piano in their flat. But somehow, by the time she married my father, my mother had taught herself to play. My father bought her a piano – a Broadwood upright from Harrods – and, when I was very small, paid for her to have some lessons. I remember a Mr Easthope calling at the house, the signal for me to be ushered out of the way by Nanna.

I've inherited much of my mother's music. There is a volume of Mendelssohn's piano works inscribed 'To Elsie, with love from Heather', with a date '24th December 1937'. Elsie was my mother and that date was her twenty-first birthday. Heather was a girlhood friend, who later married a Canadian serviceman and emigrated. The Mendelssohn pieces are not the kind of easy stuff you'd give to a beginner. Elsie had evidently become quite a competent pianist by the time she was twenty-one – seven years before she married. There are also volumes of Beethoven and Schubert from 'The Home Series of the Great Masters', piano arrangements of *Eine Kleine Nachtmusik* and of a couple of the better-known Bach Chorales, piano selections from *Iolanthe*, *The Gondoliers* and *Showboat* and the sheet music of some songs by Ivor Novello. I can't find Schumann's *Scenes from Childhood* – perhaps my sister has got that one – but I remember my mother playing some of the pieces.

I have still got her copy of Sullivan's 'The Lost Chord', which I learned to play and sing as a teenager. At the time it seemed a wonderful discovery and I would sing it over and over again. I grew out of that.

And then there are hymn-books. Before a recent house move I cut down a bit on the collection of hymn books. I had acquired a few of my own in the course of my schooldays. My mother loved to play and sing hymns. So did I – I still do – and so did my sister. The three of us had difficult relationships with each other. Some, perhaps all, of our happiest times together were spent at the piano, with one of us playing and all of us singing.

One of the pieces my mother played was the slow movement from Beethoven's 'Sonata Pathétique'. Eventually I learned to play it too. One day when I was practising my father said to my mother, 'When I first heard you play that, I never imagined that one day we'd listen to our daughter playing it.' That piece has continued to have a special place in my heart.

We were used to hearing my mother play the piano and rarely, I'm sorry to say, thought of paying her any compliments. Daddy didn't play at all, or so we thought, until one day he sat down at the instrument and gave a performance of 'Chopsticks'. We were bowled over. 'Daddy! Didn't know you could play the piano! That's really good!' He smiled modestly, while my mother went quiet.

I had my first piano lessons at the age of five or six. Although we weren't Roman Catholics I was, at the time, a pupil at a convent school. My piano teacher was a fierce old nun. When I arrived for my second lesson she asked me if I had practised. I hadn't. I'd forgotten all about it. She was very cross and sent me away without a lesson. That didn't happen again, so I suppose I must have practised a bit but I don't remember enjoying it at all and I didn't make much progress during the year or so that she taught me. After that, having come home one day and horrified my mother by asking for a rosary, I was sent to boarding school.

My new piano teacher, Miss Ross, was less frightening than the nun but I still wasn't an especially enthusiastic pupil. Miss Ross put me in for Grade One and seemed surprised when I passed with merit. I was surprised too. A year or so later she put me in for Grade Two, which I passed without merit. When I turned eleven and moved up into the senior school, Miss Ross continued to be my piano teacher. We started working on the pieces for Grade Three. But there was a problem, caused by the fact that

I, like all my friends, was very keen on swimming. The school had an outdoor, unheated pool. We weren't allowed in until it had been 60 degrees Fahrenheit for three consecutive days. If they had let us, we would have broken ice to get in there. To my dismay I found that my class's swimming time clashed with the time I was scheduled to practise the piano. I pointed this out to someone in authority, hoping they would change my practice time. No, it was tough luck, I would just have to miss swimming. There was no way I was going to do that. I missed piano practice almost every day. No one caught me. I failed Grade Three.

By the time I found out, I had left that school and was waiting to start at a new one. We were changing schools partly because my sister was unhappy. I had been quite happy at school and was fed up about it. Learning that I'd failed a music exam didn't improve my mood. I told my mother that I wanted to give up the piano. She said no. I argued and I lost. I'm grateful to her for putting her foot down.

Another new piano teacher: Miss Cox. She was young and I liked her. Knowing that I'd failed my last exam, she may have regarded me as a challenge. I began to enjoy playing the piano. The ethos of the school helped too. A charismatic head of department had succeeded in making music the thing that everyone wanted to be good at – more so than sport. This was fortunate for me because I was completely hopeless at sport and in with a chance where music was concerned. I managed to get into the school choir. I took up a second instrument, the violin, so I could be in the orchestra. And I did my piano practice. When I first went there, the school didn't have a swimming pool. That may have helped too.

When I passed Grade Four Miss Cox was as pleased as I was. If high fives had been customary in those days, we would have done one. I began to work even harder, sneaking into an empty music room, if I could find one, to do extra practice. At home I campaigned, successfully, to have the piano put in a different room from the television, so I could play it whenever I wanted to. By now an adolescent, I found that music was a satisfying way to express my emotions. I explored the music stool and taught myself to play and sing things that hadn't been put in front of me by Miss Cox (this was 'The Lost Chord' phase I referred to earlier). I can't resist mentioning that I got distinction for Grade Five. I remember the day the results were announced. A girl from my school had won the prize for getting the best mark in the whole country for Grade Eight piano.

Music exams were stressful – much more stressful, for me, than academic ones. After my Grade Five triumph I decided I wasn't going to do any more of them. What was the point? I wasn't going to take up music as a career. I just wanted to enjoy it. I regret that decision now because I'd like to be able to tell you that I passed Grade Seven, which I probably could have done, though I'm not sure about Grade Eight. I went on having lessons with Miss Cox until I left school. Soon after that she left to get married but we're still in touch.

I didn't play the piano much while I was at university. I taught myself to play the guitar. Once I'd understood that you had to forget you could read music and just learn the chord shapes, I was surprised to find how easy it was to learn enough to accompany a huge number of songs. I didn't foresee that this new skill, or my ability to play the piano, would ever help me to earn a living. However, when I began work as a primary school teacher, they turned out to be very useful indeed.

In those days every primary school needed someone to accompany the singing in assembly and to take some class music lessons. I say 'in those days' because I've no idea what happens nowadays. Do schools still have assemblies? Does the national curriculum allow any time for class music? Anyway, back then a teacher with even a little bit of musical training was a valued commodity. I still sometimes dream that assembly is about to begin, I haven't practised the hymn and it's going to be a humiliating disaster. Occasionally my attempts to sight-read my way through a hymn tune were embarrassing. Mostly I managed to stick to a repertoire of easy ones that I could play. As time went on, I introduced some folky religious songs that I could accompany on the guitar.

And I gradually worked my way into a position where I was doing more and more class music teaching. Some years I didn't have a class and just taught music through the school. I had a piano in my classroom and could play as much as I liked at lunchtime and after school. But I didn't use the piano much in singing lessons. It's easier to keep an eye on forty children while playing the guitar. And the music inspectors encouraged this, saying it was better to teach a song by singing it and that a quiet accompaniment was more appropriate than bashing out a four part harmony on the keyboard.

Those music inspectors, employed by the late lamented Inner London Education Authority, were an inspiration. I went on courses where, as well as learning new songs, we worked in groups to compose our own music, with a view to enabling our pupils to be composers too. I found this work tremendously stimulating. A supportive headteacher gave me the funds to assemble a wonderful collection of tuned and un-tuned percussion instruments. The children enjoyed themselves and discipline was no problem because they knew that anyone who messed around wouldn't be allowed to play an instrument. One day some boys found an old piano that had been dumped somewhere in the neighbourhood. The head and the school keeper wheeled it into school and the school keeper dismantled it. We ended up with a horizontal piano frame on wheels. It was brilliant. You can make fabulous sounds on exposed piano strings. We bounced ping-pong balls on them. We stroked them with sticks, spoons and strings of beads. It was loud. The tolerance of teachers in the surrounding classrooms was astonishing.

When I gave up teaching to be a freelance writer I missed the children and I missed the music. I couldn't have a piano in my first-floor flat, so I bought a touch-sensitive electronic keyboard. It was a lot better than nothing. Then, as now, I had phases when I played a lot and phases when I didn't play at all. In the playing phases I mostly go back to the same old pieces – a certain Mozart sonata, one of the easier Beethoven sonatas, some easy Bach – and polish them up again. Eventually I inherited my mother's Broadwood upright, which lives in my study on the ground floor. When we moved last year, we couldn't face trying to get it upstairs to the living room. Our new home is an end-of-terrace house, with a nice neighbour who is out at work five days a week. That means I can play without disturbing anybody except my partner, who can hear me from his study on the top floor. He has always been positive and kind about my piano practice, just as my father was about my mother's. Having her piano here plays a big part in making this place feel like home.

But it is a responsibility. I'll finish with a poem I wrote about that.

THE DAMAGE TO THE PIANO

You can barely see
the damage to the piano
where the new bookcase knocked it
but all hell would break loose,
if my mother were here.

I sit for several minutes,
pondering the silence
where I am cast adrift
with all this furniture
and no-one to tell me off.

Talk commissioned for Radio 3 in 2012

My English Teacher

Miss Bell (not her real name) was an unpopular teacher. Some girls loathed her, some just didn't like her much. I was in the latter category. If you'd talked to the girls who loathed her – or said they did – they would have told you that she was a lesbian, that she stood too close to them and touched them and they found her revolting. I don't know how many of them were genuinely bothered by Miss Bell's sexuality and how many were taking their cue from others and enjoying the opportunity for a bit of drama.

It must sound like straightforward homophobia. However, our Latin teacher, more mannish than Miss Bell, was generally assumed to be a lesbian (no one said 'gay' back then) and we were all fond of her. In fact, she was one of the most popular teachers in the school. What explains the difference? They were both good at teaching their subject. But the Latin teacher was a likeable personality with a sense of humour and she wasn't touchy-feely with the girls.

Miss Bell did not have a likeable personality, nor, as far as I can remember, a sense of humour. Other teachers were occasionally indiscreet enough to let us know that they didn't like her any more than we did. There must have been some damage, way back, that caused her to have difficulty in relating to other people.

When I was a teacher I came to understand that the crucial thing was to like your pupils – or, as I sometimes put it, 'There has to be enough love to go round.' Every now and then I came across a pupil I couldn't like, with the result that the pupil and I both had a difficult time. I don't think Miss Bell liked us. And who can blame her? Who can say which came first – her dislike or ours?

She joined the school at the beginning of the year I took my O levels. After a few weeks there was a bit of a scandal because she left a notebook lying around in which she had written about all the girls she was teaching. It included details about their home backgrounds, their characters and their abilities. A few people were upset and a lot of people made a drama out of it. I can't remember – if I ever knew – what it said about me. But I do remember her saying to me during a lesson, 'I'm told you're very clever but I haven't seen much sign of it so far.'

That worked. I made up my mind to show her just how clever I was. I began to take trouble over my English homework and was rewarded with marks that showed I had made my point. Taking trouble over homework involved reading the texts carefully and thinking about them and coming up with ideas that were not second-hand. As I said, she was a good teacher.

I opted to do English A level, which meant two more valuable years of being taught by Miss Bell. She made sure we really got to know the texts. I still know most of *Hamlet* off by heart. But the way she talked about them could be a turn-off. Going on and on about 'the rank sweat of an enseamèd bed' wasn't a good idea. However, I was on her side when a girl complained she had ruined the story by mentioning that Hamlet died at the end.

One time I gave in to the urge to parody the way she talked about poems. 'Rich' was one of her favourite words: 'This is so *rich* in adjectives.' In an essay about a poem by Keats I wrote, 'This poem is rich in adjectives, nouns, verbs, adverbs and prepositions.' After she'd marked it, she handed back my English book without a word. Then she turned to the dimmest girl in the class and held out her book. 'Not a high mark, Angela, but at least *you've* got a soul.' That didn't upset me. It still makes me laugh.

The time came to think about university. English had always been my best subject. Miss Bell told my parents that I shouldn't go to university because I wasn't scholarly enough. This was a shock. I got good marks, I came top in exams. How dare she? The history teacher was nice and had a high opinion of me. So I decided to apply to read history and got into Oxford. It turned out I wasn't scholarly enough, didn't enjoy it and didn't do well. In my late twenties, after a few years of psychoanalysis, I began to want to learn things and wished I could afford to go back to university.

Several years after I left school I heard that Miss Bell had had a nervous breakdown, after declaring that she was in love with the headmistress – a strange choice of love object for anyone. She retired and died in the 1990s.

By then I had published two books of poems. They were well publicised, so Miss Bell was probably aware that I had grown up to be a poet. I'll never know what she made of that. Most likely she found it annoying.

Areté 2013

First Teaching Job

London Borough of Newham, September 1967. My first job was in a junior school, where I was given a class of thirty-eight second-year children – I think that would be Year 4 in today's terminology. My colleagues told me that it was known to be a difficult class.

Later on, I learned that the headmaster hadn't been thrilled to have an Oxford graduate assigned to his school. It is possible that he chose that class for me in case I needed to be taken down a peg or two.

And so it was that I met Wally Johnson. In those days, you could be called Wally and not be laughed out of the playground. Johnson wasn't his real surname – I was advised to change it just in case, against all odds, he has grown up to be a *Times Educational Supplement* reader.

Wally was the naughtiest boy in the class and the bane of my life. One day I kept him behind and asked him – in classic, well-meaning new-teacher fashion – why he behaved so badly. He just stood there, looking very sad, and said nothing. After a while, arrangements were made for him to spend some of his time working at a table outside the headmaster's office.

I shall remember Wally to the day I die. I wish I could remember all the others, but most of the names and faces are lost. There were, of course, lots of nice girls ('Like your shoes, Miss. Like your handbag'). The girls were concerned when they found out I didn't have a television. 'Miss,' one of them said, 'if you got a job, you could save up and buy a telly.' I didn't have the heart to explain that I had a job already.

The school was formal and traditional and, in some subjects, I was given a syllabus. That's why, one day, I was telling them a story about Moses, probably not very well. A girl put her hand up. 'Miss, I don't get it. Is the Israelites the baddies?'

'No,' I heard myself reply. 'The Egyptians is the baddies. The Israelites is the goodies.' It was hard to stick to 'correct' grammar when it felt more polite somehow to talk like the children.

I found their East End usage attractive, though I couldn't always understand them at first. A boy tried to tell me about his father's 'barrer'. He had to say it several times before the penny dropped. 'His barrow!'

Another linguistic memory concerns the time I said a very bad word in front of my class. This was on a morning when I was having the usual little discipline problems. A young window cleaner appeared and began work on the outside of the classroom windows, observing everything with a huge grin on his face. It was too much. After the bad word came out, I clapped my hand to my mouth. 'Sorry. I shouldn't have said that.' The children reacted very well – I think their opinion of me had just improved.

We survived the year, class 2C and I, but it wasn't easy. I had to buckle down and do things the headmaster's way – old-fashioned and formal, instead of the trendy, progressive way I'd been taught in my year at training college.

By the end of it, he and I had begun to like and respect each other. The next year, I got a lovely class and was allowed a bit more freedom. My second year of teaching was the best of my whole career.

Times Educational Supplement c.1983

Green and Good for You

When I was at junior school in the 1950s, most of the poems we read were addressed to dear, innocent little souls who believed in fairies and loved to contemplate the beauty of nature. Poetry was like cabbage – green, good for you, and not very interesting.

When I was a primary school teacher in the 1970s and 1980s, my colleagues and I were able to introduce our pupils to a very different kind of poetry. It didn't talk down to them or preach at them. It didn't exclude urban and suburban children. Sometimes it made them laugh, because they recognised the people, the places, the incidents, the feelings, the dreams that they found in the poems. It showed them that lives like theirs were interesting enough for poetry, and that helped to convince them that poetry was interesting enough for them.

Of course, some likeable poems for children existed in the 1950s but there was nothing like the wealth of first-rate stuff that is available to young readers nowadays. The new poetry for children is one of the most important developments in recent English literature. Since much contemporary 'adult' poetry is too difficult for most adults, readers of all ages may find that children's books are the places to look for poems they can understand and enjoy. There is no such thing as a poem that is only suitable for children. If it's bad, it is unsuitable for everybody. If it's good, there is no upper age limit.

Faber & Faber catalogue 1993

Ted Hughes in the Classroom

Very early on in my career as a primary school teacher, I read Ted Hughes's poem 'View of a Pig' to a class of eight- and nine-year-olds. Some of them may have enjoyed it but what I remember is that one little girl had to leave the room and lie down because the poem had made her feel sick.

That was the only bad experience that came of using Hughes's work in the classroom. The good experiences, over a period of fifteen years, were many and various. Hughes's importance and distinction as a children's author are overshadowed by his other achievements – the more so because many literary people have a dismissive attitude to children's books. In primary schools – where I sometimes had colleagues who hadn't heard of Larkin or Heaney – Ted Hughes has been a big name for the last thirty years, for reasons that have nothing to do with his books for grown-ups.

The Iron Man was first published in 1968, not long after I began teaching. As I read the opening pages, I recognised that this was going to be a hit with my class. On the first page there is a compelling description of the Iron Man, employing similes that relate the giant to a child's world – his head is 'shaped like a dustbin but as big as a bedroom', his eyes are 'like headlamps'. The reader doesn't have to wait for the action to begin. On the second page the protagonist topples over a cliff and falls to bits. In a marvellous passage on the fourth page the bits start putting themselves together again: 'But as soon as the eye and the hand got together the eye looked at the hand. The hand stood up on three fingers and its thumb, and craned its forefinger like a long nose. It felt around. It touched the eye. Gleefully it picked up the eye, and tucked it under its middle finger.' I read *The Iron Man*, a chapter a day, to several classes, always in tough inner-city schools, and they always loved it. As the book's popularity grew, I read it less often, because last year's teacher had usually got in first.

Of Hughes's poems for children, the one I used most often was the quatrain called 'Moon-Hops'. It begins, 'Hops are a menace on the moon, a nuisance crop' and ends, wonderfully, with this long line: 'Clip-clop at first, then flip-flop, then slip-slop, till finally they droopily drop and all their pods pop.' I don't know what becomes of moon-hops in today's primary schools but back in the era when creativity was a buzzword, they were a stimulus for work in art, dance, drama and music. I've still got, somewhere, a tape of a child reading the poem, while the rest of the group do interesting things with xylophones, cymbals and woodblocks.

Doing this kind of work with children helped me discover a creative side of myself. I began writing poems, and aspired to write better ones. As I worked at it in my spare time, I often thought about my favourite Ted

Hughes children's book, the collection of stories called *How the Whale Became*. The creatures in these stories practise becoming what they want to be. 'The ones that wanted to become lions practised at being lions – and by and by, sure enough, they began to turn into lions.' Some creatures, such as Donkey and Hyena, don't practise being what they want to be. They merely dream about it, and have to settle for less. When I caught myself practising to become a couch potato or a workaholic teacher, it was salutary to remember them.

I reread the book recently, while editing an anthology of bedtime stories. The one I chose to include is *How the Elephant Became*, the story of a clumsy, unhappy creature who becomes a hero, and then disappears into the forest. 'Ask any of the animals and they will tell you: "Though he is shy, he is the strongest, the cleverest and the kindest of all the animals . . . We would make him our king if we could get him to wear a crown."' It was never easy to read that paragraph aloud. But it probably doesn't do any harm for children to see their teacher getting out her handkerchief at the end of an especially moving story.

'The Epic Poise: A Celebration of Ted Hughes' 1999 (edited by Nick Gammage)

Every Single Person

'Every single person has some talent,' said the prime minister in an interview for the first Open College broadcast on Channel 4. I used to work for a headmaster who said that several times a week. One of my keener colleagues discovered that a boy in his class had a special talent for long-distance spitting and tried, in all seriousness, to persuade the child to demonstrate his skill in assembly. Luckily the star spitter was too sensible to agree.

Spectator 1987

A Nice, Polite Patient

I was in analysis five times a week from 1973 until 1983. After a gap, I began seeing my analyst again at times when I was finding life difficult. By the time I moved out of London in 1994 I didn't need to do that any more, although I have continued to visit him two or three times a year, just to say hello.

I am grateful to the late Russell Twisk for ringing me up on a Friday in 1986 and persuading me to write the Listener *article by Monday. It has since been reproduced in more than one book and it led to my friendship with Stephen Grosz, at that time just embarking on his career as a psychoanalyst. He is now well known as the author of the bestselling book* The Examined Life. *Stephen is co-author of the last piece in this section, 'Analysis and Creativity'. After he had interviewed me, we both worked on the text.*

I've also included a paragraph from a letter to another friend, the author D.M. Thomas, which turned up in my archive. In the days before I had a computer I didn't usually keep copies of my letters. This one would have been written on an Amstrad word-processor. Either I liked it enough to print a second copy, or I never sent it.

Learning to Be Myself

I liked my new analyst from the first moment I set eyes on him. A balding, middle-aged American, dressed in a dark, baggy suit, he clearly had no interest whatever in being trendy. He seemed kind, honest, and trustworthy – a good man. Through all the battles that were to follow, I never seriously doubted that this was so.

It was just as well that I took to him, because the circumstances in which we began working together were far from ideal. The previous year, desperate for some help but unable to pay much out of my teacher's salary, I had applied to the London Clinic of Psychoanalysis, where the fees vary according to the patient's income. After a diagnostic interview, the clinic agreed to take me on. My condition was described, in a letter to my GP, as 'fairly severe chronic depression'. I had to wait a few months before I was assigned an analyst, but I felt better already, just to know there was hope.

Then came the false start. My first analyst was a trainee, working under supervision. After I had been seeing him for three months, he decided not to continue with his analytic work. Not my fault, I was assured repeatedly. There was concern at the clinic about the possible effect on me of losing my analyst, especially as my father had died less than two years earlier. I was designated a 'casualty' and given a more experienced analyst, the American, a classical Freudian. It was, I think, understood that he was taking on a difficult job.

To begin with I was well behaved. Still very much the obedient child, I was anxious to work out what the rules were, do everything right, and be the best patient ever. Five times a week I arrived punctually, lay on my back on the couch, did my best to free-associate, and avoided looking at the shrink. Somehow, in the course of my first analysis, I had formed the impression that you weren't supposed to say 'hello' or 'goodbye', so I didn't. I just shuffled in and out of the room with downcast eyes.

One day he commented on this. It was funny, he said, that I never looked at him. Didn't I ever feel like sitting up for a while or walking round the room? I was horrified. Certainly not. It was against the rules, wasn't it? Perhaps, he suggested, you should try it some time.

Weeks, maybe months, later, I did. I sat up and looked at him and nothing terrible happened. Next day, I didn't lie down at all. I sat there and chatted to him, just like a normal person, and I liked it. It was all much more friendly and relaxed. He let this go on for a few days before mentioning that maybe, now the barrier was broken, I should lie down for a bit and free-associate. I didn't feel like doing that.

'Is it a rule? Have I got to?' I said.

'Well, the general rule is that most of the time the patient should lie on the couch.'

'What if I don't? You can't make me.'

'Nope,' he replied, as neutrally as possible, 'I guess you'll just go on sitting up for a while.'

It was ages before I lay down again. Several times every session, he would say to me, 'You should lie down,' and I would smile gleefully. I was getting a real kick out of being bad.

Gradually I became more daring. Sometimes, instead of sitting on the couch, I would go and sit on a chair at the other side of the room. I took books out of his bookcase and read what was written on the flyleaves. I wandered around and had a look at what was on his desk.

The adult part of me was aware that he was maintaining a delicate balance between approval and disapproval. I knew that he knew that this disregard of 'the rules' was a good thing. If he'd been too benign, however, I might have felt the need to do something worse. There may have been times when he was genuinely worried that the analysis was becoming a bit too unconventional – I couldn't be sure. Occasionally I threatened to do something really bad, like taking all my clothes off or not paying the bill, but it never came to that.

What did eventually emerge, along with the innocent mischief, was a lifetime of repressed aggression. In my adolescence I had been afraid to fight with my parents, for fear of killing my elderly father. As I grew bolder, the poor old shrink copped the lot. From being an excessively nice, polite patient, reluctant to say the word 'bald' in case it hurt his feelings, I developed into a harpy, who hurled at him any and every insult that came to mind. Over the years I called him fat, old, boring, ridiculous, stupid, incompetent, a fascist, a philistine, a thick Yank who couldn't use the English language properly, and much, much more. I regularly accused him of wasting my time and money, completely failing to understand my problems, and ruining my life. By now an aspiring writer, I made a special song and dance about his ignorance of contemporary poetry, culminating in a spectacularly vicious outburst on the day I discovered he hadn't heard of Sylvia Plath. It was the final straw, I was never coming back, I was going to go to the clinic director and tell her he was useless and ask for a different analyst.

I don't, now, think it would have mattered all that much if he hadn't heard of Shakespeare either. What mattered was that I was learning, in a way that must sometimes have been very disconcerting for him, to be myself. In time, as well as finding out how to be horrible, I also learned to flirt with him and be seductive and, most difficult of all, to tell him I loved him. Towards the end of my analysis, the insults became a joke – the nastier the remark, the more it made us laugh. Nowadays, when I go back and see him, we both seem to be laughing all the time.

In the space available I have only been able to provide the merest glimpse of what went on over ten years. I still have problems, I still get depressed sometimes, I am still neurotic. But when people ask me, 'Did it work?' I answer 'Yes.' I am much happier than I could possibly have been without it.

Listener 1986

Don't Worry About It

Dear Don,

Thanks very much for your nice note. I'm glad you liked the poems. If they are OK, I shouldn't worry about all the other garbage, should I?

My analyst has helped too. I don't see him very often these days but I felt I had to go and discuss the question of sex in my book and he was quite funny about it. 'Oh God,' he said. 'Oh Jesus. Eleven years in analysis and you're feeling guilty about sex.' I said I was worried about my unconscious motivation. Was I, perhaps, advertising my sexuality? 'Yes,' he said. 'Don't worry about it. It might work.'

Letter to D.M. Thomas 1985

This was in the run-up to the publication of my first book of poems.

Freudian Mistake

The programme I intended to review this week was *Freud: For or Against?*, shown on Channel 4 at 11 p.m. last Wednesday. I was fairly sure I'd be home in time but, to make absolutely certain, I programmed the video to record for an hour beginning at 22.00. As I walked through the front door at ten minutes to midnight, I realised my mind had played one of those little tricks that Freud understood so well. My analyst says the programme was wonderful.

It is unlikely that I'll ever make the same mistake when I am aiming to record *L.A. Law* (ITV). As it happens, the shrink is rather keen on *L.A. Law* as well. He likes the blonde attorney called Grace – the one who went off with a gorilla at her wedding a few weeks ago. My favourite is Victor, in spite of his earring, but Victor doesn't seem to have any girlfriends and I think he is probably gay. I master my disappointment by telling myself that he is too young anyway, lives on the wrong side of the Atlantic, and, furthermore, doesn't exist. It goes to show, I hope, just how mature and realistic a person can be after a few years in analysis.

Spectator 1987

Analysis and Creativity

When I went into analysis there weren't any questions about whether it would be bad for me as a writer because I wasn't a writer. I was completely inhibited, paralysed really. I wanted to be a writer when I was a little girl but I'd forgotten all about it. What happened was that quite quickly, within a few months, I began writing. I was getting in touch with some powerful feelings and I didn't know quite what to do with them. One afternoon I felt like writing a poem. I'll tell you what the important thing was – it was to do with my feeling that I had a right to my own way of seeing things. Up until then I had allowed other people to impose their view of things to such an extent that I didn't very often see things for myself.

The first breakthrough was to understand that I was entitled to my view of what was going on between me and the man I was involved with. I didn't have to accept his view and I didn't have to argue with him either. I was entitled to have my own view privately, which was not the same as his. I found that I wanted to write it down and that was, I think, the first poem I wrote.

Incidentally, there's a point I want to make because

I know that feminists worry about psychoanalysis, and I have certainly had some concerns myself. One thing analysis has done is make it a lot more difficult for men to exploit me and I would imagine that's true for quite a few women. So whatever your worries are about your analyst's theories about women, if in practice it has become a lot more difficult for men to exploit you, then that is a gain.

Being able to see things for myself, feeling I was entitled to my way of seeing things, was also very much bound up with getting in touch with my feelings, with my emotions. I imagine that very often in the early stage of analysis the patient says: 'No, I'm not angry – that would be unreasonable.' At a certain point I realised, and this was a revelation to me, that when someone asked me how I felt about something, I was coming up with a plausible answer but actually I didn't really know how I was feeling. I asked myself what would be reasonable. I thought I was telling the truth but then I realised that's not how I'm feeling, that's just what I think. I began to see that I did not actually know where to look for the answer to the question, 'What are you feeling?'

I didn't know that if you accidentally drop a cup of tea over someone it may mean that you're angry with them. Once you understand that, you notice what you're doing, and you notice what thoughts cross your mind. And those are clues and then you get better at it. I think I'm pretty well in touch with my feelings most of the time now. I don't usually have to wait till I drop something to find out that I'm angry.

I want to tell you about an afternoon when I sat in Battersea Park, looking at a tree. It was as if this was the first time I'd been able to see a tree. How I felt about that tree, I realised, was mine and nobody could argue me out of it. It was an important moment, very moving. I sat there crying, and later that day I wrote a poem about the tree.

Truth to feeling is the important thing and that is why I don't see how analysis could make anyone a worse poet. Poetry is about telling the truth. The poet and the psychoanalyst are both seekers after truth.

Another parallel between analysis and writing poetry is that you have to be prepared for surprises. I think it was Robert Frost who said that there's no point in starting a poem if you know how it's going to end. It's a commonplace among poets that a poem takes on a life of its own. You have to be prepared for things to come up and for the poem to go off in a completely different direction from the one you're expecting. And it's the same in analysis – you learn to expect surprises. You don't know what's going to come up and there's the same kind of excitement.

Some people are afraid that analysis or psychotherapy will make them more ordinary and boring. There's a problem about the word 'normal'. Some analysts, I think, use the word to mean perfect mental health. But to a lot of people 'normal' means ordinary and boring. They don't want to be normal, they want to be special. In fact, of course, if analysis helps someone to be more herself it'll make her more special.

THE JOURNEY

The journey was difficult at first
Until I shipped my oars,
Let the river sweep me on,
Lifted my eyes from the dark brown water
And the search for rocks,
Saw the land, the sky, glide past.
My boat will complete the journey.
I do not know where the winding river leads.
I do not ask who will arrive.

I do not look downwards
As I reach the waterfall –
Midstream and faithful to the current.

There is no wind –
Only the power of the water.

I wrote this poem during the first year of my analysis.

Interview with Stephen Grosz, Institute of Psychoanalysis
News 1996

A Man in One's Life

Apart from a few paragraphs for children, and a 350-word contribution to a charity book, the first item in this section is the only piece of prose fiction I've ever managed to finish. As I said in my introduction, I had completely forgotten about it and was astonished when my editor told me I'd written it (after she found it in my archive). It is a feminist fable, very much of its time, which was probably the late 1970s. I had been on a course about gender stereotyping in children's books.

Ladies Do Not Rescue Princes

Once upon a time there lived a prince who owned a beautiful white horse. His name was Florizel. He was rich and handsome and he rode far and wide looking for a lady beautiful and good enough to be his wife.

One day he arrived in a small village and stopped by a well, because his horse was thirsty. There, drawing water, was the loveliest girl he had ever seen.

Now it so happened that this young lady, Miranda by name, had always dreamed that one day a prince would come riding by on a white horse and carry her away to be his wife.

Their eyes met, and in that moment both felt their dream had come true.

'Excuse me,' said Florizel, 'could you tell me the way to the inn?' To himself he said, 'I think I am in love.'

'It's just around the corner. My father is the innkeeper.' She blushed. To herself she said, 'My prince has come at last.'

Florizel stayed at the inn for three days and at the end of that time there was no doubt in his mind. He asked Miranda to marry him, she accepted, and her father gave his consent. They would travel together to

Florizel's castle and send word when all arrangements had been made for the wedding.

Towards the end of the third day Miranda packed a few belongings, mounted the white horse with her prince, and rode off into the sunset.

As they trotted along Florizel told Miranda the story of his life – of the places he had visited, of his fights and adventures – how, in the land of the Green Wizards, he had slain the dragon who lived in the swamp, and how he had rescued the King of the Elves from the dungeon in which Wandor the Wicked Wizard had imprisoned him.

Miranda was enthralled by these stories. When Florizel paused she began to think of all the things she wanted to tell him about – how she loved to walk in the woods and make friends with the animals, about the rabbits she had rescued from iron traps and cared for until they were well enough to go free again, about the birds who came and sat on her windowsill and sang to her every morning.

She started to speak, but Florizel wasn't listening.

'Look!' he exclaimed. 'There's a deer!' And he reached for the bow and arrow he kept strapped to the side of his horse.

'No! Don't shoot it!' cried Miranda. Florizel took no notice, and placed an arrow in his bow. She grabbed hold of his arm and held on to it until the deer had disappeared into a clump of trees.

Florizel was very surprised.

'All princes hunt deer,' he said in a lordly voice. 'If you are going to be a princess you mustn't try and stop me.'

'Oh,' said Miranda, and she looked thoughtful.

As they continued along the road Florizel told Miranda

more about himself – about his father, the king, and the castle they lived in, about the games he used to play as a boy. Miranda thought of more things she wanted to tell him, but somehow, every time she began, he seemed to change the subject.

'All my life, Miranda,' he said, 'I have dreamed of meeting someone like you. A beautiful girl who will sit in my castle in a long white dress, and work at her embroidery, and listen to the stories of my adventures when I come home.'

'Sometimes,' said Miranda timidly, 'can I come on your adventures with you?'

Florizel was very surprised.

'That is not what princesses do,' he replied. 'You can stay home where it is safe and comfortable and do your embroidery.'

'I don't like embroidery.'

'All princesses do embroidery,' said Florizel firmly.

'Oh,' said Miranda, and she looked thoughtful.

Miranda gave up trying to tell Florizel about herself.

'Perhaps,' she thought, 'I can't expect a prince who has had so many thrilling adventures to want to hear about the life of a village girl.' But she felt cross.

The prince was busy looking around for another deer to shoot and he didn't see what was ahead of them – a great big hole in the road.

Miranda saw it.

'Florizel,' she said, 'Florizel!'

'Hush, my darling. I'm looking for deer.'

Miranda put her hand on the reins and tried to steer the horse, but Florizel had them too firmly in his grasp.

Forward the white horse trotted until, suddenly, he too saw the hole and came to an abrupt halt on the edge of it. At that very moment a black cat, startled by the sound of hooves, leapt out of the hole and scampered away. The horse, startled in his turn, gave a great 'Neigh' and reared up in fright. Miranda clung on for dear life, but Florizel, caught off his guard, was thrown off the back of his steed, right over the hedge and out of sight.

Full of terror at what might have become of him, Miranda rode to the hedge and peeped over.

He was alive all right. She could see that. His arms and head were waving about wildly as he tried to get to his feet. But his feet were nowhere to be seen because his legs were buried in the bog he'd landed in.

'Are you hurt, my prince?' she called out to him.

'No, no. I'm not hurt. I'll be out of here in a moment.'

'Don't worry, my love. I will rescue you.'

'Ladies do not rescue princes,' said Florizel, managing to sound quite lordly in spite of his undignified position.

'Oh,' said Miranda, and she looked thoughtful. 'He will never get out of there,' she said to herself. 'How can I help him? If I walk across and try to pull him out I will just get stuck myself.'

Then she had an idea. She unwound the long girdle from around her waist. She tied one end to the horse's bridle and made a large knot in the other end, so it would be heavy enough to throw to Florizel. Then she called out to him.

'Florizel! Here! Catch this!'

'No,' shouted Florizel stubbornly. 'Ladies do not rescue princes!'

He remained sitting in the bog, and looked up at the sky as if to say, 'I will soon think of a plan.'

'Don't be silly. Here! I'm throwing you the end of my girdle. When you're tired of sitting there you can pick it up and your horse will pull you out.'

The knot landed a few inches away from the prince. For a while he sat there and pretended to ignore it, but eventually he said, 'All right. I suppose I may as well let the horse pull me out.'

He took hold of the knot. Miranda turned the horse round and guided him slowly along the road.

'Pull hard! There's a good horse.' As the animal strained and pulled she whispered words of encouragement in his ear, as she had so many times before, to creatures who were injured or frightened, or to tired carthorses outside her father's inn.

She looked backwards and she saw Florizel's feet emerging from the bog. A little further along the road, and he had been dragged as far as the hedge. With a sigh of relief she pulled on the reins to stop the horse. She threw her arms round his neck.

'Good boy. Good boy,' she whispered in his ear.

Through the hedge came Florizel, mud-spattered and cross. As he staggered towards Miranda she could not help but laugh.

'Oh, Florizel! You do look funny.'

'I am not sure,' he said, as he reached his horse, 'that you are going to make a very good princess. Princesses do not laugh at their princes.'

Miranda suddenly felt furious.

'And I am not sure,' she said, 'that I want to marry

a prince after all. Especially a prince who doesn't know when to say thank you.'

For a few moments they stood glaring at each other. Then Miranda turned on her heel, gave a last pat to the beautiful white horse, and began to walk back the way they had come.

And a bedraggled Florizel stood there and watched her, too astonished to utter a word.

What became of these two? Did Florizel find himself another lovely maiden to be his bride? Indeed he did. Her name was Flora and she too had always dreamed of a prince on a white horse. She was good and quiet and listened to all his stories and worked at her embroidery and never complained. To tell you the truth, she sometimes felt just as cross as Miranda had, but whenever that happened she said to herself, 'I have married a handsome prince. I am happy.'

And she went on with her embroidery so fiercely that quite often she pricked her finger.

And Miranda? Miranda went and lived by herself in a cottage in the woods. She had many friends – men and women and children and animals, and they loved to come and visit the cottage and talk with her. And she ate what she liked, and she wore what she liked, and she did as she liked, and she lived happily ever after.

Unpublished late 1970s

On Being Single

There are worse things than being single, and I have tried quite a few of them.

It's worse to be in a relationship with someone who doesn't love you, and makes you feel insecure. It's worse to be with someone who adores you and to be fed up with them. It's worse to be with a non-negotiator – someone who assumes that the relationship will be conducted entirely on his terms, and who couldn't care less about being fair to you. Perhaps I should stick an 'or her' into that last sentence, so as to be fair to men. For all I know, there may be female non-negotiators too, but my love affairs have all been with persons of the opposite sex.

Although I had a lot of relationships that didn't work out, I didn't make the mistake of getting trapped in any of them for very long. I've sometimes been puzzled by couples who broke up after ten years or more. How did it take them so long to notice that they didn't get on with each other? I've had flings and romantic involvements that lasted ten days, ten weeks and ten months. My longest failed relationship took just over a year. I discovered at quite a young age that being in a bad relationship is lonelier than being alone. Some of the happiest and most productive times of my life came when I was between relationships.

At a certain point I decided to avoid them altogether for a few years. I knew I had problems that were getting in the way of my finding one that would work. I was seeing a psychoanalyst, and thought it would make sense to wait until I had sorted myself out. At the same time I was influenced by the Women's Movement (this was in the early 1970s), and considering the possibility that having a man in one's life might not be such a great idea anyway.

It was around this time that I began to write poems. In fact, one of the first poems I wrote was about the relationship I was in when my analysis began. The man had his view of what was going on between us, and I had been allowing him to impose it on me. One day I understood that I was entitled to my way of seeing it, which was different. I also understood that I didn't have to have a shouting match with him – I didn't even need to tell him. I just wrote it down on a piece of paper, and it was safe. We broke up not long afterwards.

Deciding to give up on men for a while was a huge relief. It provided the space I needed to concentrate on reading and writing poems. I had a full-time job as a teacher and it was difficult to fit in the job and a man and the writing. Still in my twenties, I hadn't given up on the idea of settling down and having children eventually. Many years later I laughed a lot when I read the New Year resolutions at the beginning of *Bridget Jones's Diary*: 'develop inner poise and authority and sense of self as woman of substance, complete without boyfriend, as best way to obtain boyfriend'. I recognised that there had been an element of that in my quest to develop my writing.

By the time my first book was published, I was forty. The 'no relationships' phase was over well before that. If you like sex, things happen. And, of course, I was worrying about the biological clock. Quite a few of the poems in *Making Cocoa for Kingsley Amis* are about love affairs. The book got a lot of attention, my literary career took off, and that was when being single became really difficult. I gave up my job to be a freelance writer. Any anxiety I had about doing that was focused on money. What I didn't foresee was how much I would miss the daily contact with my colleagues and pupils.

As a self-employed writer living alone in London, I was very isolated. I had two close relatives still living and I didn't get on with either of them. My friends were busy with work and children, and many of them lived in distant parts of the metropolis or outside it. During this period, I was away from home quite a bit, doing poetry readings in this country and abroad. When I was in London I was often out at literary parties. The trips and the parties were good but I hated going back to my silent, empty flat.

My second book, *Serious Concerns*, was written during those years. Although much of it is humorous, it is an unhappy book. The most perceptive review of it (by Robert Nye in *The Times*) said that it was written 'out of deep despair'. When it was published, I had to give interviews and make a big effort not to come over as sad.

The truth was I had got to a point where I couldn't see how I was going to go on, if I couldn't find someone to share my life with. I needed someone to be on my side when I got a bad press and to be pleased for me when good things happened. I needed someone to know what was going on in my life, and talk with me about the little everyday things. You can't go to a book launch and tell people about your problems with the washing machine (although, at my worst, I probably did).

I felt that I could manage without a partner if I had a relative or friend to share a home with but I couldn't think of anyone who was likely to fit in with that plan. My friendships were under strain because I needed so much more from my friends than they could reasonably give me, and I was often angry with them. When I read upbeat articles about single women enjoying their freedom and the company of a group of close, supportive friends, I wondered what I was doing wrong. I had plenty of CSFs when I was in my twenties and I suppose I had just got into the wrong age group. To survive as a single woman in middle age you need to be part of something – a workplace, a church, a village or small-town community. A man can become a regular in his local pub but I can't see that working for a woman.

In my mid-forties I had a whirlwind romance and got engaged to a man who talked about us having children, which might just about have been possible. It seemed to be the fairy-tale ending I had longed for, but it turned out to be a big mistake, and lasted only four months. After that, it was hard to pick myself up. I read *A Life of One's Own* by the psychoanalyst Marion Milner (writing under the pseudonym Joanna Field). She describes keeping a diary in which she mentioned only the things that gave her pleasure each day. I tried that and found it helped me to live one day at a time and to realise that my life wasn't all misery. It was an exercise that has proved to be of lasting value because it left me with an improved capacity for enjoying small things – a flower, a meal, a conversation in a shop.

Then, when I had completely given up hope, I met the man I have been living with for the past twelve years. I took one look at him and wanted to make him happy. As it turns out, I can do that, and he can do the same for me. I was forty-eight when I moved in with him – too old to have children. That is a sadness, but not a tragedy because everyday life with love in it has been like walking into the sunshine from a long, dark tunnel. I am a lucky woman.

The Times 2005

Getting Married

We both had reservations about marriage. On my side there was some feminist suspicion of the institution. On his side there was his divorce. As the years went by it looked more and more likely that we were going to stay together for the long run. Perhaps it was safe to make those solemn promises and feel confident that we'd be able to keep them.

On the other hand, we were fine as we were. Now and again we'd agree that we should get married for practical reasons, and then do nothing about it. We were busy. We couldn't be bothered.

With the advent of civil partnerships, I became more and more concerned that we didn't have the legal rights that were now granted to gay couples. We both liked the idea of a civil partnership. You can just sign a document: no need to have a ceremony or any fuss or expense. And you don't, if I understand the matter rightly, have to make a solemn vow to stay together until one of you dies. I learned this by asking the local authority. It was difficult to get a straight answer out of them, almost as if they wanted to keep it quiet.

People said, 'Why don't you just get married in a

register office?' They didn't understand the difference. My solicitor didn't understand the difference. Our hopes were raised when civil partnerships for heterosexuals were initially included in the gay marriage bill. But the proposal was dropped. The government said there was 'no call' for them. Every time the prime minister told us about his strong belief in marriage, I shouted at the television set, 'Fuck off, Flashman!'

A year ago we gave up and decided we'd have to have a wedding. By this time we had been together for nineteen years. I asked his grown-up children if they would mind if we did it very quietly, without inviting the family. Yes, they would mind. They wanted to be there. If they were there, we'd have to invite other close relatives as well. The whole idea – from finding a dress to arranging the catering – seemed too much.

Then my wonderful friend Adèle came to the rescue. 'A wedding! It will be great. It will be fun. I'll make a cake.' I cheered up. My partner and I set a date, booked the register office and told the family. I found a dress and took it round to Adèle's house for her approval. I ordered party food from Waitrose and champagne from Tesco. I began to look forward to it. I spent the best part of an afternoon on the internet looking at paper napkins for the reception and several more hours choosing flowers and negotiating with my future husband about the music.

The day arrived: 8 May 2013. We had twelve guests at the register office – ten family members plus Adèle (whose husband was sadly too ill to be there) and one old friend of the bridegroom. It was a lovely occasion.

I was in tears as I made my vows. Afterwards we walked home with our guests, through a beautiful part of Ely, and started on the champagne.

We like being married. We're surprised to find we are even happier together than we were before. We find it amusing to call each other husband and wife. The other day my husband said he was glad we were married, rather than civil partners. And I'm very content with things as they are. Even so, I think we should have had a choice. There are heterosexual couples who want civil partnerships and I'm still on their side.

Guardian 2014

A Mark on a Piece of Paper

The first two pieces in this section give differing accounts of how I began to write poems. They are both true, although neither is the whole truth. One factor that isn't mentioned in either piece is my work as a teacher, which involved reading poems with children and encouraging them to write.

Concerning the poem about Roger Bear: I have confessed, in the opening piece in the book, to copying the first line from the girl in front. To be strictly accurate, it was the brown/town rhyme that I copied. The uninspiring adjective 'lightish' was my own contribution.

The rest of this section includes some pieces about writing poems and some about life as a writer. The two interviews were conducted by email, i.e. the answers were written by me, not the interviewer. My thanks to Sam Gardiner and my student Boyana Petrovich, who provided the questions.

First Poems

My earliest poem, written when I was six, was about my teddy, Roger. 'Roger Bear is a lightish brown,' it begins, 'He makes his home in Teddy Town.' I am not ashamed of this opening couplet, although I would look for a stronger adjective than 'lightish' if I were writing it today. From line three onwards, however, the poem goes downhill and I shall refrain from quoting any more. Only one or two trusted friends have been allowed to study the full text of 'Roger Bear'.

Nobody at all has ever read my next efforts, the terrible poems I wrote when I was fourteen. For a long time I almost managed to forget about them myself. I have often told people that I didn't write during my adolescence, and if my lines on the marriage of Princess Margaret came to mind, I dismissed them as not really counting. But they are still extant, neatly copied out into a little notebook, along with some passionate stuff about a pop singer whom I was definitely going to love for ever and ever and an angry outburst entitled 'On the Arrival of My Report. Dec 21st 1959'.

After that, fortunately perhaps, there was another long silence. In 1967 I wrote a poem about a sunset and put it in an envelope. Six years later, tidying a cupboard one Saturday afternoon, I found it and thought it wasn't bad. Having nothing better to do, I sat down and wrote another poem, then another and some more the next day.

I began to read a lot of poetry and, with growing excitement, to explore the process of creating it. Working on poems, I discovered, made me happy. In the past, however hard I worked at my job as a teacher or at anything else, I had always suffered from a feeling that I hadn't found quite the right way to use my time or ability, that something was being wasted. I imagine that many people have this feeling and that some of them never find out what it is that they really want to do. I was lucky because finding out is more than half the battle.

It wasn't, of course, quite as simple as this account makes it sound.

There were several reasons why I was ready to begin writing in the early Seventies – living alone for the first time was one of the most important. The old poem in the cupboard was just the trigger. I am glad I kept it.

Bookcase 1986

A Book That Changed Me

'Few books today are forgivable.' If I were to read *The Politics of Experience* for the first time now, that opening sentence might be enough to put me off. There is much else in R.D. Laing's book that makes me smile at the younger self who took it all so seriously.

But back in 1973 it was the right book at the right moment, five months after I had entered psychoanalysis. In the course of those months I had begun to discover feelings I hadn't acknowledged before, with the result that I was more alive, more curious, and better able to concentrate on what I read. This was an exhilarating phase of my life but it wasn't an easy one. There was a lot of anger, fear and grief to deal with, and at the same time I had to carry on teaching for a living.

A passage on page 34 of *The Politics of Experience* gave me the courage to try a new way of dealing with powerful feelings: 'If I draw a pattern on a piece of paper, here is an action I am taking on the grounds of my experience of my situation . . . What intention have I? Am I trying to convey something to someone? Am I amazed that something is appearing that did not exist before?' When someone writes a poem, Laing says,

'Through all the contention of intentions and motives a miracle has occurred. There is something new under the sun.'

It occurred to me that there was no reason why I shouldn't make a mark on a piece of paper. It needn't be seen or judged by anyone. I found some paper. I wrote words on it. By the end of the afternoon there was paper everywhere. I gathered the sheets and stacked them neatly: the drafts of my poem.

Perhaps only those who have been timid, over-obedient children will understand why I couldn't write before. It wasn't just page 34 that helped: the book clarified the importance of believing in my own experience, despite the attempts of others to invalidate it. For all its stylistic flaws and pretentious bits, *The Politics of Experience* is more than forgivable. I never met Dr Laing but I cried when I heard that he was dead.

Independent on Sunday 1991

On Failure

I felt a failure at junior school because I was no good at games. Secondary school was better because the important thing there was to be good at music. I wasn't hopeless at that, just average. I managed to get into the choir, which, far more than the first lacrosse team, was the élite. All this time I was doing well academically and, as I rose through the school, that began to seem less irrelevant. I got into Oxford. I left school feeling OK about myself.

That soon changed. I spent three years in Oxford feeling like a complete loser. I put it like that because it is less painful than saying, 'I was a complete loser,' which is, I suppose, the truth. Here I have paused for a long time, wondering if I can bring myself to write about it. I don't think I can. I became very depressed. For the first and last time in my life, I seriously considered suicide. For years after I graduated I couldn't go into the centre of Oxford because it held too many painful memories. I can go into Oxford now but not into the memories. It looks as if this attempt to write about failure is going to fail.

However, the reason the editor of *Areté* asked me to

write this piece had nothing to do with my experience as an undergraduate. After Oxford I went into primary school teaching and, a few years into my teaching career, began writing poems in my spare time. It was a long time before anything of mine got published. How, he wonders, did I deal with this period of failure? For a long time it wasn't a question of failure because getting into print wasn't the point. At university I taught myself to play the guitar. I didn't expect it to lead to a career in music – I just felt like doing it. Now I felt like reading and writing poems. It was some time before I thought of trying to publish them. A colleague who wrote poetry himself asked to look at them, thought they were promising, and told me about some magazines I might try. My response was to go out and buy a box of paints. I knew that no one would ever tell me I was any good at painting.

The idea that poems of mine might be published was pleasing but I was afraid that if I got focused on that it would spoil the whole thing. Worrying about impressing editors would corrupt and inhibit me. None the less, I gave in to temptation and began sending out poems. For six years nobody accepted anything. And, yes, that did get me down. Why was I spending all this time and energy on writing when I wasn't getting anywhere? Before I tried to publish, of course, this question didn't arise. I was writing because I wanted to. Now and then I would decide to give up but I found that I couldn't. The only excuse for being a poet, I sometimes say, is that you can't help it.

I went on Arvon courses and usually came back with

renewed determination to work at my writing. At a certain point I decided that writing better poems was my priority – more important than my teaching career – even if none of them ever appeared in print. It may or may not have been a coincidence that it wasn't long after this that a couple of editors began accepting my work.

You have to want to do it for its own sake, I tell aspiring poets. I have observed that people who are too focused on getting published and recognised tend not to achieve either. I still have to struggle to rise above concerns about what editors and reviewers and other poets will think. Some of my best poems are written when I get into a mood where I just don't care, where I can say to myself, 'They'll all hate this but I'm going to write it anyway.'

I write a poem and, often enough, I have to acknowledge that it's not much good. I imagine all poets have to live with that kind of failure and I guess that many of them remember Samuel Beckett's advice: 'Fail again. Fail better.' I publish a book and it doesn't get shortlisted for any prizes. That's a different kind of failure. I have to convince myself that it doesn't matter. In her biography of Sylvia Plath, Anne Stevenson suggests that Plath wasn't clear about the difference between artistic success and worldly success and that this was part of her problem. It is a crucial difference and poets need to understand it.

Areté 2012

Decadence and Virtues

'You're very brave,' people keep telling me since I decided to give up my full-time job. They mean reckless and I often wish they'd stop frightening me with their congratulations.

It's not as if I've gone the whole hog and started drawing the dole. Since September 1984 I've been half a primary school music teacher and half a freelance writer – not as difficult as being half a fairy and half a mortal, like Strephon in *Iolanthe*, but I haven't resolved the identity problem yet. One Thursday morning, a couple of weeks into my new life, I bumped into an old school-fellow in the local bookshop. I hadn't seen her for years and she asked what I was doing these days. 'I'm, um, a writer,' I replied, without much conviction. She looked sceptical and began talking about her children.

Of course, I shouldn't have been in the bookshop on a Thursday morning – I should have been at my desk. It's astonishing how much time can be filled with vital errands when the alternative is a long stretch of tearing out one's hair over a notebook or typewriter.

Then there's housework, which, as Stevie Smith pointed out, is a wonderful excuse for not doing anything else.

I try to resist the temptation to clean and tidy the flat every morning, silencing the demon inside me that says it will be easier to work when I've got things straight. A poet friend of mine recently lost two days of her working life because she gave in to the feeling that it was time to tackle the ingrained dirt on the kitchen floor. I've sworn that the ingrained dirt on my kitchen floor is staying right where it is until my collection of poems is in the bag.

Among the advantages of working at home are the cheap and easy journey – approximately twelve paces along the corridor to my study – and the fact that there is no need to bother with make-up or the search for un-laddered tights. I can stay in bed until nine o'clock and be at my desk by ten past, telling myself firmly that I am not going to get up and clean the window or make another cup of coffee just yet.

The first hour is usually the worst but on bad days the morning can seem very long and lonely. Twelve o'clock is dinner-time at school. Should I let it be dinner-time at home as well? Or should I press on for another hour and listen to *The World at One* while I eat?

Once one has stopped, there is the problem of getting started again. Quite a few writers of my acquaintance are aware that *Woman's Hour* is a remarkably good programme nowadays. One or two know all about the early afternoon television shows. I'm not yet decadent enough to switch on the box in the daytime – the very idea of it terrifies me almost as much as those more famous evils of the freelance writer's life, the drink and the debts. I've given up keeping sherry in the kitchen cupboard and am determined to run my personal finances on Thatcherite lines, never spending money I haven't got. Except on essentials such as cigarettes.

Perhaps it is just as well that I have to change myself back into a teacher on Sunday night. Primary school teachers lead virtuous lives – they have to, to stay on top of the job. No late nights, no hangovers, no long lunches, and never a moment wasted during the working day. Two and a half days a week of this regime reduce the danger of my going down the long slide into drunken idleness. And they serve as an effective reminder to keep the type-writer busy – or it will be back to the nine o'clock bell and school dinners five days a week.

Poetry Society Newsletter 1985

We Pay You Fifty Pounds!

Home from lunch. Three messages on the answering machine. Good. Two are from friends, the other – not so good – is from a television producer. Am I interested in being on his chat show? Oh dear, I thought they'd given up. Most offers of work make my heart sink but this kind is the worst, so I've developed some rules for dealing with terrifying opportunities.

1. Don't say no until you've found out the details.

2. Don't ask other people for advice because they'll tell you to say yes.

I ring back. The producer tells me a bit about the programme and I don't like the sound of it. He mentions that he would like me to be lively. 'No,' I say firmly, 'I'm not lively.' He takes my word for it and goes away.

Sometimes what they want you to be is bouncy. This once caused me to sit in almost total silence through a live radio programme. Every time I thought of something to say, I paused to consider whether or not it was bouncy enough, and failed to get my oar in. Fortunately one of the other guests, a nineteen-year-old American hula-hoop champion, was coming on like Tigger, so the producer got what he wanted. If it's bounciness you're after,

American hula-hoop champions are a much better bet than poets.

That producer never asked me to do anything again, but he omitted to warn his colleagues. Every so often one of them rings up and has a go. The reason they ask me, despite there being no evidence whatsoever of my having any talent for that kind of thing, is that I am female. 'We thought it would be nice to have a woman on it,' they say. Really advanced producers don't just want *a* woman, they want *some* women. And it seems that few of us are willing to take the risk. Sometimes they ask me for suggestions. How about X? 'We've asked her already.' Y? 'No, she won't do it either.'

It just goes to show how sensible we are. Unless you've got something to sell, there really isn't much point in being on chat shows. The money? It isn't enough to buy a dress to wear for the occasion. Radio is a slightly better bargain because you can look as scruffy as you like, but nobody gets rich by doing it. When I implement rule three: ask how much they're going to pay you, producers sound a bit shocked. After a great deal of umming and erring, they eventually come up with an approximate figure, making it clear that this kind of sordid detail isn't really their business.

The assumption is that people will jump at the chance to be on radio or television – especially television – just for the sake of it. A while ago I was approached by one of the producers of the Comment slot on Channel 4. I said there was nothing I wanted to comment on at the moment but that didn't put him off. He told me what you had to do and when you had to do it. 'And the good news,' he added, 'is that we pay you fifty pounds.'

'Are you serious?' I asked.

'Yes, yes,' he assured me. 'We really do pay you.'

'Are you serious,' I persisted, 'in suggesting that fifty pounds for all that work is good news?'

'But you're on television,' he reminded me. 'You get famous.' Oh yes, terrific. You get famous and then, presumably, you have even more wallies ringing you up and trying to persuade you to do silly things for peanuts.

Of course, it must be said that not all producers are wallies, nor are all programmes silly. I have sometimes enjoyed taking part in radio programmes and have even, once or twice, sat in front of a television camera and survived. It can be OK if it's pre-recorded and the subject is something both you and the presenter know about. It helps if there are no hula-hoop champions on the same show. It helps even more if there is absolutely no requirement to be lively or – another favourite word in this context – bubbly. I think I'll keep a whistle by the telephone and blow it down the ear of the next person who rings up and invites me to bounce.

Guardian 1990

The Struga Poetry Festival
20–24 August 1987

I very much enjoyed my visit to Struga. The place is beautiful, the hotel was comfortable, and my room had a balcony with a wonderful view of the lake and the mountains. We were able to swim and to relax in the sunshine. On the Friday we were taken on a boat trip across Lake Ohrid, given an open-air lunch, and visited a very pretty old monastery near the Albanian border.

The poetry festival was not as badly organised as I had been led to expect. By and large, events began on time. The main problem was that the organisers were not very good about letting us know what was happening. On the opening evening, for example, Carol Rumens and I had some difficulty in finding out whether or not we were supposed to be reading. At the last minute we were told that Britain was to be represented at this event by Brenda Walker and that we would be reading on the bridge on Sunday evening.

The bridge over the River Drim at Struga is a lovely setting for a poetry reading and thousands of people came to listen. Forty-four poets took part, reading one poem each. Actors read Macedonian translations of all the poems by non-Yugoslav authors. The event lasted about two hours and I only understood five poems. We had not been given a running order, so we had to listen for our names to be called, not knowing whether we would be next or have to wait another hour. Fortunately my name came up quite early and after that I could relax. I felt sorry for the poets who read towards the end.

This was the only event I was asked to take part in at Struga. The two events I most enjoyed attending were the reading by Australian poets – I was particularly glad to discover the work of Vicky Raymond – and the evening in honour of Tadeusz Różewicz, winner of this year's Golden Wreath, which took place in the Cathedral of St Sophia in Ohrid. Our hosts provided us with an English translation of Różewicz's speech.

I was reliably informed that the symposium on Poetry and Language was not very interesting. A brief visit to one session confirmed this impression.

Informal contacts with other poets were more stimulating. I was able (thanks to their knowledge of English) to talk with delegates from Germany, France, Belgium, Denmark, Russia and Czechoslovakia, as well as with the Australians and the one American. Struga reminded me what a limitation it is only to know one language – one of the things I have gained from the trip is a determination to work at my schoolgirl German.

Our contacts with Yugoslavian poets were somewhat complicated by the fact that we are women. Women were very much in the minority at this festival and ordinary politeness on our part was sometimes misconstrued by hopeful Macedonian males.

On the Monday the poets were scheduled to give readings in other Macedonian towns. It was difficult to find out which town we were supposed to be going to and what time the buses were to leave. I ended up in Prilep, where I was asked to read three poems in the town square. One of these was then read in a Macedonian translation. Nobody laughed at the jokes but I hadn't expected them to. After the reading we were given a splendid meal on the balcony of an old monastery overlooking the town. It made a very pleasant last evening.

Some of the poets involved in the festival were understandably disappointed that there was so little opportunity to read their work and that, despite continual assertions in the speeches that poetry is wonderful, important, sublime etc., nobody seemed very interested in their actual poems. Several visitors expressed the view that the festival has grown too large and that the format needs rethinking. It seemed to me that the organisers were barely aware of Carol's or my existence. However, I didn't really mind. I decided to take the view that it was generous of our hosts to put us up and feed us for five days and to expect us to do so little in return. The trip was a welcome break and it did me good.

Report for the British Council 1987

A View of the Rockies
Teaching in Colorado Springs, September 1999

Thursday afternoon

Hello darling,

I thought I'd sent you some news in a fax, so I don't have to try and squeeze it all into a phone call.

I am living in a big apartment with a balcony and a view of the Rockies. It's the top floor of a pretty old house – I mean the house is both old and pretty. I'll take a photo to show you. There is a telephone here and the number is 000 0000000. Apparently if I'm out you eventually get through to a voicemail service in someone else's name (a previous occupant presumably). Don't leave a message – I don't know how to retrieve it. We are 7 hours behind the UK.

Dave Mason has been great – I'm horribly dependent on him at present but I'm hoping this will change as I find my way around. I have now found out how to call a cab, so that should help.

The flight was fine – I quite enjoyed it. It's very hot here. That doesn't stop people jogging at midday – madder than mad dogs and Englishmen.

I've been making a few enquiries about activities here. Can you guess what a natatorium is? Win Coll. has one under a different name.

I've also been to the chapel – very loosely based on Winchester Cathedral but aiming more at a Chartres effect inside, with lots of dark blue glass. I looked at the notice board to find out about services and this is what it says.

Monday
6–8 p.m. Zen Buddhist

Tuesday
6.30–8.30 Fire Weed Sangh
8–9 NA Group

Wednesday
7–9 Tibetan Buddhist

Thursday
6–7 p.m. AA Group
7–8 p.m. Kundalini Yoga

Sunday
12–5 CC Community Kitchen
6–7 AA Group

I kid you not. I have found an episcopal church not far away and I'll go there.

Sorry about my writing. I'm leaning on my knee. I haven't been to my office yet but I may be able to type future faxes. I'm still jet-legged, of course, but not at all headachy despite travel and altitude.

Talk to you soon.

Lots of love

W.

Sunday lunchtime

It was good to speak to you this morning. After that I went to the episcopal church and liked the service very much. It was mostly very familiar. Apparently the rector is keen on the Anglican tradition. It's encouraging to find enthusiasts for the Anglican tradition over here. I felt at home but that reminded me that I'm a long way from home. It was moving. The only unfamiliar bit was when they struck up our national anthem and sang their words to it. I have to say it seems a bit of a cheek to call the tune 'America'. I had a good mind to sing 'God save our gracious green'. But I didn't.

It finished in time for me to go on to the Interfaith Service outside the college chapel. I quite liked that too. I was sitting on a small rock, so I was glad it didn't go on too long. There were refreshments afterwards and I introduced myself to Bruce the chaplain and his sidekick, 'the chapel intern'. I think I may get roped in to take part in a series called 'Faculty and Faith', where I have to discuss my faith with students.

Uh oh. Anyway it helped to pass what could have been a lonely morning.

This afternoon I'm going to see a colleague about my syllabus. And I'll probably have a look at the poetry section in the library.

I feel that this is the calm before the storm. Tomorrow I meet my students and start work. Everyone says it is 'very intense' – I can't see that it can be all that intense when we only have to teach in the mornings and it is understood that 'the students will need a break' in the middle of that. But I am a bit nervous.

Thursday 2 p.m.

Hello, my love. I'm just waiting for the car rental firm to ring and tell me if they can come and pick me up, so I thought I'd take the opportunity to scribble a few words to you.

Thanks for your phone calls. I'm OK here but it would be harder if we weren't in touch.

The sun has come out again today. There is snow on Pike's Peak, as I may have mentioned earlier. The trip to the Garden of the Gods with my students was very enjoyable. Wonderful to think I am being *paid* to sit in the sun in a beautiful place and wait for someone to bring me a poem. One of them, Carlos, wrote something that brought tears to my eyes. It was about different gods – Mexican, American Indian, Greek – with Jesus and the Virgin coming in towards the end. A couple of the others didn't really write anything, but you can't win them all. Different exercises work for different people.

Tonight I'm going to a concert of medieval Spanish music. I'm looking forward to that.

I'm thinking of driving down to New Mexico when the teaching is finished. Someone told me Santa Fe and the country around it are well worth seeing. 19 days till I come home. Lots of love, W.

P.S. The car is a Nissan Altima (big) automatic with a CD player. I'm pleased with it.

Faxes to Lachlan Mackinnon 1999

If I Don't Know

A perceptive reviewer of my last collection, *Serious Concerns*, observed that it was written 'out of deep despair'. This one wasn't. Life got better, and I became even less prolific than I used to be. In 1999 someone told the *Sunday Times* that I had stopped writing. They printed this information without bothering to check it. I didn't really mind but it wasn't true. Most years since 1991, when my last book went to press, I've produced a handful of poems. There were times, admittedly, when I thought I was just too contented and boring to write any more. One day, when I had been feeling entirely convinced of this, I was surprised to find myself writing the poem I've called 'Being Boring'.

It occurred to me that 'Being Boring' would make an eye-catching and daring title for the whole book. My publishers said it was too daring and they were probably right. Anyway, although the idea amused me, I decided that an amusing title might be a mixed blessing this time round. It's difficult enough to get the world to notice that my poems don't all have jokes in them. So I settled for 'If I Don't Know', the title of a poem about wandering around the garden on a beautiful evening in June.

The garden comes into half a dozen other poems in the book. Here I have paused for a long time, trying to think of some more generalisations to make about the contents. There are a few love poems, one or two humorous items about the opposite sex, and three poems about paintings – two paintings I quite like and one I dislike intensely. As in my earlier books, there are some poems about poetry and poets, none of them, this time, by Jason Strugnell. There's a sequence of short poems called 'Traditional Prize County Pigs'. These are not about poets or about men. They are about pigs. There's a poem about socks. There's a poem about a confirmation present. And some others, about this and that. You will have gathered that this is not a book with a theme.

The last poem is a twenty-two-page narrative called 'The Teacher's Tale'. It is fiction but it draws on my experience as a London teacher. I began teaching in 1967, when my central character would have been six years old, and continued until the 1980s. The story is in rhyming couplets, which turned out to be more difficult than I expected. The going was sometimes very slow. I cheered up when someone told me that Milton only managed twelve to fifteen lines a day when he was working on *Paradise Lost*. And he didn't have to think of rhymes.

Poetry Book Society Bulletin 2001

Jason Strugnell is a poet I invented. He was the author of several poems in my first and second books.

Is Life a Comedy?

Interview with Sam Gardiner, Dream Catcher *magazine*

SG: Your *Making Cocoa for Kingsley Amis* was a tremendous debut (in 1986), and you became famous overnight. How did this change your life? How did Wendy cope?

Wendy: I had already given up my full-time teaching job and was working part-time. When the book came out I was suddenly in demand to do all sorts of things, so I gave up teaching altogether. Ever since then I have been able to earn a living without having a job. For this I am eternally grateful.

However, the overnight fame, modest though it was compared with what happened to, say, J.K. Rowling, was difficult to deal with. The telephone never stopped ringing, I couldn't keep up with the post, and every day brought new demands and decisions. I had to toughen up very quickly and learn to say no. I wished there was someone I could talk with about what was happening to me but in those days I didn't know anyone who'd had a similar experience.

SG: Has your poetry changed over the past twenty years? If so, what do you think are the main differences?

Wendy: Since *Making Cocoa* I've done fewer parodies and literary jokes. In my early work I only used rhyme and metre in humorous poems. Now I use it in some (though not all) of my unfunny poems as well. My second book, *Serious Concerns*, is a very unhappy book because I was unhappy when I wrote it. My most recent book, *If I Don't Know*, is calmer and more contented.

SG: Your poetry is often meaningful in that it deals lightly with serious subjects. Do you consider yourself a serious humorist?

Wendy: I'm a poet with a sense of humour. Actually I've hardly ever met a poet who didn't have a sense of humour but many of them keep it out of their poems. I do believe that humour and powerful emotion can exist in the same poem. And that a funny poem can be saying something important.

SG: Laughter is one of the distinguishing characteristics of humanity, especially that we can laugh at ourselves. Do you see yourself as a custodian of one of humankind's precious endowments?

Wendy: No.

SG: One objection to humour is that life is not a comedy, but do you agree that life is a comedy, or at least a tragicomedy, once you get the joke?

Wendy: I think that humour often arises out of misery and despair. Sometimes life seems so terrible that all you can do is laugh. To see life as anything other than a joke, and to care about making the world a better place, you have to be reasonably happy and optimistic.

SG: It has been said that a sense of humour is a sense of proportion. Do you agree?

Wendy: Yes, I think there's some truth in that.

SG: Do you think that people, and poets are people, often take themselves too seriously?

Wendy: My first response was yes. But on reflection I'm not sure. When I was young my self-esteem was so low that I didn't take myself seriously enough. Beginning to write was about feeling entitled to take myself seriously. But I hope I'm not self-important. Most of the poets I know have enough sense not to behave as if they take themselves too seriously.

SG: How do you self-edit, and do you agree that the wastepaper basket is a poet's best friend?

Wendy: Most of my poems go through lots of drafts. I write in a notebook and I never throw a draft away because I might want to go back to it. I never throw a finished poem away either, although I don't try to publish all of them. I have a file labelled 'Failures'. Now and again I look through it and find something that doesn't seem to be a failure after all. So, no, I don't use the wastepaper basket.

SG: Do you try to write during regular hours?

Wendy: Only when I'm working on something long, such as *The River Girl* or 'The Teacher's Tale'.

Dream Catcher magazine 2005

Very Fond of Bananas

Interview for Kingston University website

Boyana Petrovich: You sold your archive to the British Library in 2011. It included 40,000 emails, poetry notebooks, school reports, Word files, early school work, correspondence and accounts books. What struck me most was that you had all this saved in the first place. Most of us don't even keep a diary. What motivated you to collect such an extensive archive? Were there things you decided to exclude from the archive and keep just for yourself?

Wendy: I've always tended to keep letters and so on, even before I had any thought of being a published writer. When I got published I became aware that my documents might be of interest at some stage. In 2011 I needed to raise money to buy a house – my partner was retiring and the house we lived in went with his job. So I contacted the British Library. To persuade them to buy I had to throw in a few things I would rather have kept.

BP: After you published *Serious Concerns* Ted Hughes wrote to you: 'I like your deadpan fearless sort of way of whacking the nail on the head – when everybody else is trying to hang pictures on it.' That must have felt good. How would *you* describe your poetry? How would you like people to remember it?

Wendy: There's no way of answering this question without sounding boastful. I think it's for other people to describe my poems, not me.

BP: 'The Uncertainty of the Poet' is a very funny, yet deep and eloquent piece of writing – and it uses only eight different words. In an interview you said that you were commissioned by the Tate Gallery to write about any one of their exhibits. When you saw de Chirico's painting *The Uncertainty of the Poet* you thought 'I am a poet. I am very fond of bananas' and that became the beginning of the poem. How did the rest of the poem happen?

Wendy: I thought of the first stanza, then the idea of using the same words in a different order throughout the poem. Once I'd got that far, the poem more or less wrote itself.

BP: You have said that in order to become a better poet it is essential to read poetry, both contemporary and of the past. Who did you most learn from? Is there a poet (or two) you can recommend to those who find classic poetry long-winded and difficult?

Wendy: A.E. Housman; his poems are short, accessible and moving.

BP: You seem to prefer form to free verse. What is it that form offers you that free verse doesn't?

Wendy: It makes a few decisions for you and provides a template. I like having some rules to follow. But I do write free verse as well, of course.

BP: How do you know when a poem is finished? Is it a knowledge or a gut feeling? Do you ever rewrite a poem you'd thought was done?

Wendy: When I've written a poem I go over it in my head. Often I realise there is a line that needs improvement. Then there may be another one. When I stop finding lines that need improvement, the poem is finished. I have occasionally changed things many years after I first wrote them.

BP: Your debut collection, *Making Cocoa for Kingsley Amis*, has sold over 180,000 copies to date (according to poetryarchive.org), which must put you among the bestselling living poets. How hard is it to make a living as a poet?

Wendy: Nowadays many published poets have salaried positions on creative writing courses. For those who don't (and I'm one of them), it can be difficult to make a living. I'm fortunate in that my books sell well by poetry standards, although I couldn't live on the proceeds. Doing poetry readings is an important source of income for me. The teaching I do at Kingston is paid per session (not salaried) and doesn't contribute much to my income. I'm now old enough to receive my state pension, plus some pension from the years I was a school teacher. That helps a lot.

BP: At a reading you did in Hong Kong you said that 'being a person who makes a fuss about copyright has become [your] second career' and that you don't think the battle for copyright is lost. Has your opinion changed at all? Do you know that the video recording of the reading is available online?

Wendy: No, I didn't know that recording was available online. I may have been asked about it and forgotten. I'm not too concerned about audio or video recordings, as long as printed versions of the poems don't appear. Sometimes I think the battle for copyright is lost but I carry on fighting anyway. I'm not the only one.

BP: In many of your poems you talk about relationships between men and women. There's been a lot of talk about whether (at least in your poems) you hate men or not, something female feminist writers often encounter. You don't label yourself a feminist poet. Can you please tell us why?

Wendy: Back in the 1970s, if you called yourself a feminist writer, other feminists would give you a hard time if they didn't think you were feminist enough, or in the right way. If you didn't call yourself a feminist, they just ignored you, which was fine with me. I do, however, think I'm a feminist, that is, someone who believes men and women are equal.

BP: You teach poetry at Kingston University. Do you like teaching or is it something you have to do? Do you think that it in any way influences your writing?

Wendy: To be honest, I wouldn't do any teaching if I didn't need the money. However, I often enjoy it. I've been surprised how much I've enjoyed doing workshops at Kingston and getting to know some of the students.

BP: Contemporary literary theory likes to talk about the 'death of literary fiction', how it has become a pastime, just a distraction from our doom, that fiction is frivolous and inferior to reality. What's your opinion on this, both as an author and a reader? Do you think poetry is in a superior position to prose? What is the role/place of poetry in our lives?

Wendy: I read a lot of novels. I often enjoy them very much. Sometimes I come across observations about human behaviour that enrich my life.

No, I don't think poetry is in a superior position to prose. For one thing, far more people actually read novels than read poems.

And the role of poetry in our lives? I can only quote Dr Johnson, who said that the purpose of literature is to help us 'better to enjoy life or better to endure it'.

Kingston University website 2013

It's a Free Country

He was an elderly man and he had queued up with the people who were waiting for me to sign their books. When his turn came, he announced unapologetically, 'I don't read poetry. I write it. I've brought you a copy of my book.'

If he had been younger, I might not have been so polite. I smiled, took the book and thanked him. Later on a quick glance through the self-published volume confirmed what I already knew: the poems were no good. People who never read poetry don't write poems that are worth reading.

It's a free country, of course, and anyone can write whatever they like. However, if you are interested in writing well, in working at being a better poet, then the most important piece of advice that anyone can give you is that you have to read both recent poetry and the poetry of past centuries. That's how you learn. The elderly gentleman must have come across some poems at some point in order to have a concept of what a poem is. But vague memories of a few things you read at school are not enough.

It seems odd to me that anyone who hates reading poetry should want to write it at all. Are there amateur painters who never go to an art gallery? Or amateur musicians who never listen to music? Sometimes non-reading poets explain that they are afraid of being influenced. They don't understand that being influenced is part of the learning process. Some of my earliest (and unpublished) poems read like poor imitations of Sylvia Plath. Others read like poor imitations of T.S. Eliot. I was unaware of this at the time. Gradually I worked my way through these and many other influences towards finding my own voice. Nowadays I hope I sound like myself in my poems but I am still influenced by what I read, still learning.

Judging poetry competitions has reinforced my understanding of the crucial importance of authenticity of tone. If a poem is to work, the voice in it has to sound like the real voice of a real person. This applies to dramatic monologues (where the poet puts words into the mouth of another character) as well as to first-person lyrics. Some insecure people use a special voice on the telephone that sounds quite different from the way they usually speak. Inexperienced writers sometimes do something similar in their poems – using 'poetic' language that they would never employ in ordinary speech or reaching for clichés because they lack the confidence or the energy to find their own, unique way of expressing themselves.

I find that the most important and helpful question to ask myself when I'm working on a poem is 'Am I telling the truth?' T.S. Eliot said that the greatest difficulty for a poet is to distinguish between 'what one really feels and what one would like to feel'. Knowing what one really feels is not always such a simple matter as it may sound. Whether we are writing about our own lives, or our response to the world around us, or public events, Eliot's dictum still holds. If the poet is, knowingly or unknowingly, being dishonest, the poem will fail. We need to search for the words and images that accurately convey the truth of the matter.

We also need to acquire some technical skills. A few years ago I spent a month teaching aspiring poets in Colorado Springs. They all wrote free verse and knew very little about traditional forms. By the time I had finished with them they could write iambic pentameters. 'If you want to be a poet,' I insisted, 'you have to know this stuff. You don't have to go on writing like this but you should understand how to do it.' They responded very well. I especially remember the fiery young Hispanic-American and his excellent revolutionary villanelles.

They were a talented bunch and I hope that some of them are beginning to get published. They won't all be famous poets – quite possibly none of them will. I hope they won't feel the time they spent on learning to write was wasted. I've spent a lot of time learning and practising the piano, even though there was never the slightest possibility of my becoming a professional pianist. It is something I want to do for its own sake. So is writing poetry. It has to be. I've observed that people who are too focused on being published tend not to get anywhere. If you have the urge to write poems, and to work at doing it better, good luck to you. I hope you will find the journey rewarding.

Introduction to 'How to Write Poetry', a booklet published by the Guardian 2008

Battle for Artistic Autonomy

I'm going to begin with a quotation – my favourite quotation about being an artist. It's something Schubert said:

'I give to the world what I have in my heart and that is the end of it.'

Of course, doing that is not always as simple as it sounds. You have to work at finding the language to express the truth as accurately as possible. And I believe that is what I have to do as a poet. My job is to write the poems I feel impelled to write, to make them as good as I can, and to put aside all other considerations.

These are some of the other considerations that have to be put aside. Will anyone want to publish the poem? Will I want to publish it? Will anyone want to read it? Will it make me any money? Will it upset anyone? Will other poets approve of it? Those things are all secondary, and I can think about them later. Sometimes I have to promise myself I'm not going to publish the poem before I can get on with writing it. Then I usually break the promise, but not always.

I get cross if anyone tries to suggest that being a poet means I have some kind of special duty to society, other

than to write the best poems I can. As it happens, they
do sometimes turn out to be useful. For example there's
a poem I wrote about my grandmother that is used on
training courses for people involved in the care of the
elderly. I'm very pleased about that. But it wasn't the
reason I wrote the poem, and, if it had been, I doubt if
it would have been as good. That kind of usefulness
might be approved of by the politicians and administra-
tors who see the arts as an instrument for improving
society but I don't think it's any more important than
writing a poem that speaks to a lot of individuals. When
people write and tell me that particular poems of mine
have moved or helped them, I'm greatly encouraged. I'm
lucky to have readers while I'm still alive. If I didn't, I
hope I'd still find the courage to go on doing my thing,
as George Herbert did, and Emily Dickinson did, although
their poems weren't published until after they died.

I think we're expected to touch on the question of
funding. In my case it is very simple – I've never had
any. I had a job when I wrote my first book, then I found
that I could afford to go freelance. I've won a couple of
small prizes but I've never had a grant. My safety net
was that I could always go back to teaching ('was' because
I'm past retirement age now and enjoying a teacher's
pension). It is perfectly possible to combine a day job
with writing poems. Philip Larkin, to name only one,
did it all his adult life.

But I chose to go freelance. Freelance writers, of course,
are beset by threats to their autonomy. It is important
to be clear about the difference between being an artist
and being a hack. Hack work is what you do for money,

rather than for artistic reasons. I've had to do a fair amount of it but I do know the difference. Twenty years ago a wise friend advised me, 'Don't write poems for money. Do other things for money.' So I do poetry readings and the odd bit of journalism and broadcasting and judging competitions. I do sometimes accept a commission to write a poem but only if it's interesting. Of course, the work you do for artistic reasons may end up making some money – I've been modestly fortunate in that respect, and I do realise that makes me luckier than some other poets who are at least as good as me.

There's another kind of threat that isn't just about money but also about fame and recognition. After my first book came out, I was bombarded with requests to do tacky or irrelevant things for the media – panel games, chat shows, weekly poems about the news. I was new to all this and I had to make some quick decisions. What they all boiled down to was this question: now the opportunity has arisen, would I like to be a media personality instead of a poet? I did seriously consider it, and decided that I wouldn't. I turned down a lot of opportunities and I haven't regretted it. I do the occasional bit of radio, as you may have noticed, but I am selective.

It's a struggle, I find, to get into a frame of mind where I can put aside the concerns I've mentioned and write what the hell I want to write. But when it happens, the experience is wonderful, and the making of the poem is its own reward.

Speech delivered at the Battle of Ideas 2006

Price of Poetry

Sir,

One of the reasons there is 'no money in poetry' ('Cue the Pavarotti of poetry', August 12) is that it is very easy to steal from poets by using our work without permission. Schools and colleges indulge in illegal photocopying; performers recite our poems to paying audiences without even thinking about the copyright law.

When permission fees are paid, they are often very small. The fees offered for commissioned poems are frequently insulting. William Cash is quite right to say that poetry is 'absurdly cheap'. In suggesting that poetry should appear in public places because 'it would cost much less than hiring an advertising firm to come up with a banal package', he seems to me to be condoning the exploitation of poets.

Good poems ought not to be cheap. Poets don't enjoy being mercenary but we have to live. If 'shrewd promoters' and others are becoming aware of the commercial potential of poetry, then we are going to have to learn to be tough about money, and make poetry a lot more expensive.

Yours faithfully,

Wendy Cope

Letter to The Times 1991

All Rights Reserved

One summer's day, strolling through a cemetery, my partner and I had a conversation about what we would like on our gravestones. He suggested that mine should read 'Wendy Cope. All Rights Reserved'.

He knows all too well that I am obsessed with copyright. A poem is very easy to copy, whereas nobody is going to photocopy or download a whole novel or work of non-fiction. Therefore poets are especially at risk if people do not know and respect copyright law.

The authors of short, funny poems are especially vulnerable. Short funny poems have a tendency to run off on their own and detach themselves from the names of their authors. There's a well-known poem I've liked since I was quite small. 'The rain it raineth every day/ Upon the just and unjust fella/ But mostly on the just because/ The unjust hath the just's umbrella.' For decades I thought of it as anonymous. Then, when I was compiling an anthology of poems for children, I found it in the British Library with an author's name on it: Baron Charles Bowen. I was happy to reunite poem and author in the anthology. I've seen a poem by Ogden Nash in white paint on a beam in a pub with no mention of the author's name. I've seen one of mine in an anthology, attributed to Dorothy Parker. I could mention numerous other examples.

But this isn't just about very short poems. There's a problem for the authors of all poems, unless they're really, really long, like *Paradise Lost*.

A few years ago one of my stepsisters asked me about Jenny Joseph's poem 'Warning' – the one that begins 'When I am an old woman I shall wear purple'. This relative spends a lot of time in the USA and had heard about the Red Hat Society, a women's organisation inspired by Jenny's poem. As 'Warning' is included in an anthology I edited, I offered to send her a copy. 'No,' she said. 'Don't bother. I'll get it off the internet.' That was when it dawned on me that nowadays, if you want a copy of a particular poem, you don't have to buy a book.

My poems are all over the internet. I've managed to get them removed from one or two sites that were major offenders but there are dozens, if not hundreds, of sites displaying poems without permission. If I google the title of one of my poems, it is almost always there somewhere, and I can download it and print it out. I'm sure that this must affect sales of my books. I've tried googling some of Seamus Heaney's poems, and those of one or two other well-known poets, and it's the same. Authors' organisations – the Society of Authors, the Authors' Licensing and Collecting Society (ALCS) – are concerned about this problem. Publishers aren't happy either because they, too, are being robbed. But everyone agrees that internet piracy is extremely difficult to fight.

Often the offending websites are the responsibility of well-meaning enthusiasts, who have no idea that they are breaking the law. Neither do the people I meet every now and then who say: 'I liked your poem so much that I sent copies of it to all my friends.' I'm supposed to be pleased. I've learned to smile and say thank you and point out very politely that, strictly speaking, they shouldn't have done that. They should have told their friends to buy the book. Or bought it for them.

In an attempt to do something about widespread ignorance of copyright law, the ALCS and the Poetry Society commissioned me, some years ago, to write a poem on the subject. It is called 'The Law of Copyright' and the form is borrowed from Kipling's poem 'The Law of the Jungle'. Too long to reproduce here, the poem points out that 'This is the law: the creator has rights that you can't overlook./ It isn't OK to make copies – you have to fork out for the book.'

Another bee I have in my bonnet concerns literary festivals. These days they often invite actors or anthologists to come along and present a programme of other people's poems. I'd like to be sure that they have cleared permission to read the work to a paying audience, and I know that in many cases they haven't. So the people who wrote the work are getting no benefit from the event. For most poets, fees for doing readings of their own work are an important part of their income. So, if festivals invite actors or anthologists instead, and the poets are not paid for the use of their work, then poets have cause to complain.

One argument that often comes up in relation to all this is 'But it's free publicity.' Well, it's true that there are poets who are happy to see their work anywhere and everywhere, just for the sake of the attention. But for those of us who make a little bit of money from royalties and permission fees, and depend on that income, it's different. Free publicity has no value if all that happens is that even more people download your poems from the internet without paying for them.

In the long run, of course, if our poems survive into the long run, we'll be in no position to benefit from royalties or permission fees. All poets hope that their work will outlive them. I'm no exception. Even so, I sometimes feel a bit annoyed by the prospect of people making money out of my poems when I'm too dead to spend it. And I feel sad for other poets. One day I came across some postcards in a gift shop featuring poems by A.E. Housman, who died in 1936. I bought a postcard and, on the back of it, wrote the following lines. When I hear them in my head, they are sung to the tune of the hymn 'The Church's One Foundation'.

POSTCARD POEM

Will they do this, I wonder
With verse of mine or yours
When we are six feet under
And deaf to all applause?

We bring home little bacon
En route for that long night
And when the profit's taken
We're out of copyright.

Speech made at AGM of the Authors' Licensing and Copyright Society, abridged for publication in the Guardian 2007

Poetic Insight of the Year

'The reason why modern poetry is difficult is so the poet's wife can't understand it.'

Wendy Cope, quoted in the *Guardian*

Sunday Times 1992 (their headline)

Addictions, Ageing and Two Cathedral Cities

'Addictions, Ageing and Two Cathedral Cities' or, to put it another way, all the bits that didn't fit in anywhere else.

Smoking

When I left school in December 1962 I began smoking about twenty cigarettes a day. By Christmas 1984 it had gone up to thirty. During that twenty-two-year period not one day passed without my lighting up.

I worried about the risk to my health and made occasional attempts to stop. These invariably ended at around lunchtime on the first day, with me in floods of tears, convinced that life wasn't worth living anyway. Once, having tried to give up on a Saturday, I was still so appalling on the following Monday that a senior colleague told me I'd better not try again. For years I regarded stopping as a complete impossibility.

I was wrong. I last smoked a cigarette on 20 January and the past few weeks haven't been half as bad as I expected. At present my most troublesome withdrawal symptom is an unstoppable urge to share the good news and pass on theories and advice. People have been very patient – it must be especially boring for acquaintances who have never smoked a cigarette in their lives. I hope this article will get the subject out of my system and help a few smokers as well.

First of all, it was important to realise that giving up

is largely a question of self-confidence. This was originally suggested to me by Bobbie Jacobson's excellent book *The Ladykillers*, which I read three or four years ago. Men, says Jacobson, are less likely to perceive themselves as hopeless addicts and that is why more of them succeed in kicking the habit. It made sense and, although it didn't have immediate results, Jacobson's theory stayed in the back of my mind and helped when the right moment arrived.

It is no coincidence, I am sure, that my successful attempt took place at a time when I had reason to feel unusually confident about my work because my first book had just been accepted for publication. A nasty cough and pains in the chest played their part but so did the feeling that perhaps I was a person who could achieve difficult things, after all. Once I had stopped, my self-esteem improved dramatically every day and I felt radiantly happy far more often than usual. Nothing I had been told led me to expect this and I dare say it isn't so for everybody. Those of us who were sure we couldn't give up for a single day probably benefit from it more than most.

Another important difference between this attempt and the failures of the past has been a supply of nicotine chewing gum. I had known about this for some time but fear of failure prevented me from asking for a prescription. Just after Christmas, in an unusually determined mood, I made an appointment with my doctor.

The first bit I chewed tasted so disgusting that I nearly spat it out. But after about ten minutes I found I wasn't desperate for a cigarette any more – I would have liked one but I could survive. The instructions tell you to stop smoking completely as soon as you begin using the gum. This didn't work for me. I got through an evening and part of the next day before caving in at a party. After that I went into practice for three weeks, smoking as little as possible and getting by on gum the rest of the time. I proved to myself that I could manage certain activities without cigarettes – making telephone calls, writing letters, having a quiet drink with non-smoking friends.

As my confidence grew, I became more ambitious. By the time I was down to four or five cigarettes a day I began to think it might be easier to stop altogether. The final hurdle was to get through a day at the school where I am a part-time teacher. At 4 p.m. I was so pleased with myself that I felt I could do anything. I didn't light a cigarette and I haven't had one since. 'The first few days are easy. It's the second week that's really difficult,' someone had told me. This profoundly discouraging remark turned out not to be true in my case. Another friend said the second day was the worst – she had felt very peculiar. So did I. Driving home from school that afternoon I realised I probably shouldn't be in charge of a car – my concentration wasn't good enough. In the evening I tried to put a pile of song sheets into alphabetical order and couldn't remember the alphabet. I was vague, slow and slightly feverish.

By day three the very worst was over. For the next week or two the main difficulties were waking up much too early in the mornings and hunger. I have always had a weight problem and was terrified of getting fat if I gave up smoking. My experience of dieting came in useful. I ate quite a lot but I knew what to eat and it didn't get out of control. Since alcohol makes me crave cigarettes, I haven't been drinking much. So far I have lost three pounds.

The only unpleasant surprise has been a series of minor ailments – colds, laryngitis, earache. My doctor says it is a common reaction. Sleeplessness, hunger and lack of concentration ceased to be a problem quite early on. Irritability, too, is easing off. Right at the start I had had to make a firm decision about this: it is nice to be polite to friends and colleagues but it isn't worth ten or fifteen years of one's life. I don't know if I've been a lot more horrible than usual. People around me don't seem quite as nervous as they did two or three weeks ago.

It's early days yet and I'm still on the nicotine gum but I am optimistic. I find it hard to imagine any circumstances in which I would smoke a cigarette. However bad things were, it could only make me feel worse.

Unpublished 1985

Killer Su Doku

It was my partner's fault. He began doing Su Doku puzzles soon after they first appeared in the papers. He gave me a pointer or two as to how to go about solving them and I quickly became addicted.

It could have got nasty, with the two of us competing for all the available puzzles. But the advent of Killer Su Doku saved the day. Once I'd tried a Killer, I lost interest in ordinary Su Doku. We have two daily newspapers. We do our favourite puzzles and then we swap.

The difference between ordinary Su Doku and the Killer variety is that the latter involves some arithmetic. It isn't necessarily any more difficult. Both kinds of puzzle range from 'Mild' or 'Gentle', through 'Moderate', 'Tricky' and 'Tough', to 'Fiendish' and 'Deadly'. The really difficult ones sometimes drive me crazy but they are also the most fun.

The wonderful thing about these puzzles is the way they absorb my attention. If I'm feeling too anxious or upset to concentrate on anything else, they give me some time off from my troubles. And they make time fly. They are perfect for train journeys or any situation that involves sitting and waiting.

Of course, they are a terrible waste of time. A friend of mine justifies her Su Doku addiction by saying she does them to keep her mind active, so she won't go gaga like her mother. That excuse doesn't work for me because writing a poem involves at least as much mental activity as doing a Killer Su Doku. If it weren't for the puzzles, I would probably do more work. But I believe it is important to have a few things in my life that I do purely for pleasure. Killer Su Doku won't improve me and it won't get me anywhere. It just helps me to enjoy my life.

From 'Modern Delight', Waterstones/Faber 2009

I'm over this addiction now. It was replaced by Wordament, a game I play on my mobile phone. It is very addictive and not to be recommended.

Why Winchester?
Interview with *Wykeham Life* magazine

Why Winchester?
I moved here in 1994 to be with my partner, the poet and critic Lachlan Mackinnon. He is employed by Winchester College and I am freelance.

Obviously I was the one who had to move. But I'd had enough of London by then and I don't miss it at all.

If you could live anywhere, where would it be?
For quite a long time I thought there was nowhere I would rather live than Winchester. Now, I would be happy to move to Cambridge or to York or maybe to Oxford. I have interesting friends in all those places – and they are beautiful cities. Sometimes I think I'd like to move to a sunnier part of the world. At one time I wanted to live in California but I decided it isn't green enough.

If you could change anything about the city, what would it be?
Someone once said to me that the good thing about Norwich is that it has a bohemian quarter. I realised

that that is what is missing in Winchester – there is nothing remotely bohemian. Although I still think it is a pretty nice place to live, I do sometimes find it oppressively staid and respectable.

What relaxes you most and why?
I get very tense if I've got a lot of work to do. The best way to relax is just to get on and do it. And then all the obvious things – a hot bath, a walk, a bit of mindless television.

You are given a blank cheque; what would you buy with it?
A house. We live in tied housing and don't own a property.

What's the best piece of advice you have been given?
'Dare to be true', George Herbert (Anglican priest and poet 1593–1633).

And the worst?
To buy a two-bedroom flat in Herne Hill in the 1970s instead of a one-bedroom flat in Pimlico.

What is your most guilty pleasure?
Spending too much money on clothes and cosmetics.

Given a soapbox, what would you shout about?
At present I feel very strongly about the question of marriage and civil partnership. I believe that heterosexual couples should be allowed to choose between these two arrangements, rather than having to get married for the legal and financial benefits. And locally, I'd shout about the need to make Canon Street a one-way street.

What fictional character would you most like to be?
I can't think of one. I love Jane Austen's heroines but I wouldn't want to live in a world without modern medicine and washing machines.

What would you like to be doing in ten years' time?
Breathing.

One talent you wish you had?
There are two: I'd like to be a better musician and a better linguist.

Wykeham Life magazine 2007

The Water Meadows, Winchester

When I first moved to Winchester in 1994 and began walking in the water meadows several times a week, I felt as if I had come home to an England I had always loved. That it felt like a homecoming made no sense because I had lived in London suburbs during my childhood and for most of my life. Perhaps what I came home to was a vision of a perfect English landscape, glimpsed in films and on rural excursions. Here, right on my doorstep, was a landscape that lived up to the vision.

The water meadows are on the southern edge of Winchester, three minutes from the street where I live, and ten minutes from the High Street. There's a path through them that runs between two waterways: a mill-stream known as Logie, and the much wider River Itchen. On the first part of the walk, going south, there are fields and trees on the far side of each waterway, and in the distance is St Catherine's Hill. Everything, as far as the eye can see, belongs to Winchester College but the path is open to the public and its dogs.

At some point in the 1980s there was a plan to run

the M3 through the water meadows. The headmaster and some of his staff attended the public inquiry and made their presence felt by humming. It sounds to me like a risky strategy for schoolmasters: they would have been in trouble if their pupils had borrowed the idea in school. Eventually the plan was altered. Despite the best efforts of protesters, the motorway cuts through nearby Twyford Down instead.

If I listen out for it, I can hear some traffic noise on my walks, except when it is drowned by the sound from a culvert or a weir. I also hear birdsong, and, now and then, the humming wings of flying swans. And I often stop to watch the waterbirds – coots, moorhens, dippers and ducks – going about their business.

The poet John Keats stayed in Winchester for six weeks in 1819. In a letter to his brother he described his daily walk, which took him past the cathedral, and along College Street, where, although he wasn't aware of it, he passed the house where Jane Austen had died two years earlier. Then he followed the path through the water meadows all the way to the ancient alms house, the Hospital of St Cross, which is still there today. He told a correspondent that 'there are the most beautiful streams I ever saw, full of trout'. They are still beautiful and you can still see trout in the Itchen.

On his walk on 19 September Keats was so struck by the beauty of the season and the 'temperate sharpness' of the air that he 'composed upon it'. The result was his ode 'To Autumn'. It was his last great poem. Already ill, he died seventeen months later, aged twenty-five. It moves me to know that my regular walk is much the same as his, and to reflect on my good fortune in having had so many years to enjoy it.

From 'Icons of England', Think Books/CPRE 2008

Ageing

My father told me that when he was a boy he heard his father, then aged sixty, singing in the bath. He was astonished that anyone so close to death could be so happy. When Daddy told me this he was well over sixty himself, and laughing at his youthful foolishness. His first, childless marriage ended with his wife's death when he was in his mid-fifties. He married my mother when he was fifty-eight and I was born just before his sixtieth birthday. I didn't grow up with the idea that sixty was very old.

A few years after my father died at the age of eighty-five, my mother remarried and lived to celebrate a second silver wedding. On that occasion I made a speech confessing that, at the time of their wedding, I had thought the bride and bridegroom (fifty-eight and sixty-three) were getting on a bit but, now I was in my fifties, I realised how wrong I had been.

The lives of my parents helped me to understand that it doesn't have to be all over when you're forty, fifty or sixty. When I turned forty I acknowledged that I was now middle-aged but my first book was published that year and that was a new beginning. Still single, I met lots of new people and had a series of love affairs. Even so, I got depressed when I read articles saying that a woman in her forties has a better chance of being killed by a terrorist than of finding a man. Perhaps I was lucky or perhaps the articles were wrong. When I was forty-eight, I settled down with Mr Right. The seventeen years we've had together have been the happiest of my life.

When I turned sixty I threw a party in our lovely garden, with lots of champagne. I was pleasantly surprised by the number of friends who accepted the invitation, including quite a few who had to travel some distance. My partner made a speech that almost moved me to tears. It was a wonderful day. I didn't get depressed about being sixty. I felt great.

The reason I was able to afford all that champagne was that I got a very nice birthday present: my lump sum from the teachers' pension fund. From the age of twenty-two until I was forty I worked as a London primary school teacher – full-time until the last couple of years. If I'd had any say in the matter, I wouldn't have put a chunk of each month's salary into the pension fund – certainly not when I was in my twenties – but I didn't have a choice. Now, of course, I see what a good idea it was. As well as the lump sum, I began getting a monthly income – my teacher's pension and, because I was one of the last lucky women to get it at sixty, my state pension as well. I wouldn't want to have to live on my pensions but, for someone who is still working as a self-employed writer, they are a very helpful supplement.

If I'd gone on working as a teacher, I would have retired at sixty, with a much bigger pension and no work to do. Now and then, when I'm too busy and feeling stressed, I think that might have been nice. However, mostly I feel concerned about people who have to retire. When I gave up teaching I missed having colleagues and being part of something. But I was only forty and I had plenty of interesting work, new friends and acquaintances, and opportunities to travel. I wonder how I would have dealt with being cut loose at sixty, with my working life behind me.

Occasionally I have a fantasy about retiring from life as a writer. I imagine having some cards printed – or setting up an automatic email response – saying 'Wendy Cope regrets that she is unable to reply because she has retired.' I can't afford to do that because I still need to earn a living. I'm unlikely ever to have the time or resources to go on a world cruise or learn to play golf or do an Open University course in some fascinating new subject. I'm glad that other people my age are able to enjoy those things but, on reflection, I'm not too envious. When I think about it seriously, I realise that the main thing I would want to do with any extra spare time is to spend it writing.

This year I turn sixty-six. That's old, I keep saying to myself. At sixty-five you get start getting free flu jabs because you are vulnerable. You get a letter from the surgery offering you a free one-off vaccination against pneumonia. You are really getting on. Sometimes I think I should adjust to thinking of myself as an old woman. I remember a dear family friend who, in her seventies, used to talk about 'the old people', as if she wasn't one of them. We laughed at her, affectionately, behind her back. Nowadays, I find myself doing exactly the same thing.

Of course, I'm lucky. In her sixties, my mother began to be crippled with arthritis. I'm alive and I'm reasonably healthy. When I was forty-nine I had sciatica quite badly for more than six months. That made me feel old. Seven years ago I had a bad knee and limped everywhere. That made me feel old. Both conditions were curable and, once I was better, I felt younger again. I don't like to hear talk of someone being 'marvellous for her age' as if it is an achievement. Much of it is luck. When people are not marvellous for their age, it's usually the result of a health problem beyond their control.

I think it's safe to say that I am still too young to be marvellous for my age and it's impossible to know how long my luck will hold. As I've got older, I've become better at counting my blessings and focusing on the part of the glass that is full. My partner is still with me and we still love each other. I worry about his health and nag him about his lifestyle because I want us to have a good few more years together. I have interesting work and no boss – I love being self-employed. I get invited to travel abroad – last year to Sri Lanka and the USA, this year to Brussels, Italy and Hong Kong. I sometimes wonder how long I'll have the energy to do all this travelling and wish the opportunities had been there when I was younger. But better late than never.

Of course, I'm not overjoyed about looking older. It helps that I wasn't beautiful when I was young. Like Martha Quest, the heroine of several Doris Lessing novels, I've had fat phases and thin phases. I'm still aiming for another thin phase. But, at my age, looking motherly isn't a disaster. My partner loves me anyway. I do my best, for his sake and my own, but I no longer feel that happiness is impossible unless I'm thin. Botox? Cosmetic surgery? Absolutely not. Too risky, for one thing. I do use a variety of face creams, without being at all sure whether or not they make any difference. But I'm liberated from the intense anxiety I used to have about my appearance when I was younger. I'm no longer on the pull and I couldn't be more thankful.

My partner recently retired from his day job, although he, too, is still working as a writer. Free to live anywhere, we uprooted ourselves a few months ago and moved to a new city. This was hard work – for a few days after the move the pain in our backs, legs and feet reminded us that we weren't young any more. But we are finding it invigorating to have a new city and a new part of the country to explore. We have old friends in the area and we are making new ones as well. I am enjoying my life. The only sadness is knowing that it can't go on for ever. That's true for everybody but harder to forget at my age. How many years of active life do I have left? Five? Ten, if I'm lucky? I try to make the most of every day.

Daily Mail 2011

Living in Ely

Where would we like to live? We were agreed that we didn't want to stay in Winchester. Lachlan was keen to be within reach of a copyright library. A few years earlier we'd visited Aberystwyth and discovered the National Library of Wales. Lovely library. Nice place. He suggested we might move there when he retired but I vetoed that. Aberystwyth is just too far away from everything – our friends and families and most of the places I might need to travel to for work.

Cambridge. That was the next idea. We have friends there, it's within reach of London, and there is a copyright library. I began looking at Cambridge properties on Rightmove and soon figured out that we couldn't afford anything suitable. We weren't just looking for a place to live. We both need a space to work in and that meant more than two bedrooms.

Someone said, 'Ely is very nice.' I'd been to Ely a few times, on one occasion to give a talk in the cathedral. I knew the cathedral was stunning, and the area around it very attractive. I went on the internet and looked at some properties. Much cheaper than Cambridge, and only fifteen minutes away on the train.

We decided to come and spend a night here and have a look around.

Driving into Ely on a Thursday I was nearly put off the whole idea. Dreadful traffic, nowhere to park. By the end of the day I'd found out that Thursday and Saturday are market days. On the other five, traffic and parking are not a problem. And, *mirabile dictu,* all the car parks are free.

We finally found a space near the river. I'd never been to the riverside area of Ely before. We walked along, found a pub, and had a coffee on the deck outside, looking at the water, the narrowboats, the willow trees, the birds.

I was enchanted. 'If we could live in this part of Ely,' I said. 'I'd be content.'

I was aware that this part of Ely had the added and very important attraction of being near the station.

That was in May 2010. I kept reading the emails from property websites, hoping that the right house would come up. One Friday in August, there it was: four-bedroom house, affordable, near the river and the station. We rang the estate agents, viewed the house next day and made an offer. It was the only one we looked at.

One London friend said, 'Isn't it a boring place?' We don't find it boring.

We like walking by the river, or just sitting beside it and watching the world go by. To get to the High Street and the cathedral we take the path through the Dean's Meadow, enjoying what must be one of the most beautiful views in England. In the foreground the meadow, with mature trees and horses. Behind it the full length of Ely

Cathedral, with its tower and its second tower, the famous octagon. In winter we can see the top half of the cathedral from our front windows at home. In summer much of it is hidden by trees.

Ely is a small city. It used to be the smallest in England but there has been a lot of new building in recent decades and the population has doubled to 20,000 since 1981. Now it is the second smallest – bigger than Wells. The city's size makes it easy to live in. Nothing is very far away.

Three weeks after we moved here, I went by car to Cambridge. Driving home, I realised I wouldn't want to live there even if we could afford it. Too big. Too busy. After I moved out of London, I decided I was through with big cities. Cambridge is bigger than Winchester, where we lived before. Silly of me to think I'd like to move there.

We see our Cambridge friends and we have new friends in Ely. Most of them chose this place for the same reason that we did: it's near Cambridge but cheaper. All of them agree that it is a great place to live.

Ely used to be very poor. With the new building and the Cambridge overspill, it is becoming more affluent. It's also within commuting distance of London. I wouldn't want to make that journey every day but there are people in our street who do. There are plenty of nice places to eat and drink, a very good bookshop and four supermarkets. However, the rest of the High Street hasn't caught up with the new affluence.

The Isle of Ely. Until the draining of the fens it was surrounded by marshland, which was uncrossable unless a local showed you the way. After the Norman Conquest Ely held out until a treacherous monk led the invaders along a secret path into the city. The cathedral stands on a hill. Known as 'the ship of the fens', it can be seen for miles.

That brings me to another reason I was glad to move here. I've always loved the flat landscapes of East Anglia. On train journeys to the north or south of Ely I rarely read because I can't stop looking out of the window at the big sky and fields stretching for miles to the horizon. The view of Ely as you come into it from the north is captivating – as I am sometimes told by acquaintances who have never set foot in the place. You look across the river to the riverside pub and houses and, beyond and above them, the cathedral. The sight makes me feel proud: my beautiful city.

Unpublished 2014

Head in a Book

For more than a decade I had an enjoyable little job reviewing children's picture books for the Daily Telegraph *every few weeks. When it comes to reviewing grown-up books, I am much less confident and often say no. As an older woman poet once said to me: 'Women are afraid of getting it wrong.' That's certainly true of me. Here, following a piece about my childhood reading, are a few book reviews my editor and I thought worth reproducing. They include a tribute to my dear friend and mentor, the late Gavin Ewart.*

Head in a Book

My maternal grandmother, Nanna, lived with us and she taught me to read. First she taught me the alphabet, then the sounds, then how to put them together to make a word. She also read me stories. One day, I was looking over her shoulder while she read *The Buttercup Farm Family* by Enid Blyton.

'Can I try and read it myself?'

Nanna handed me the book and sat with me while I read aloud. It was no problem. I told Nanna it was OK, I could read it by myself, and she went off to do something in the kitchen. Every now and then there was a word I couldn't figure out, so I had to go and ask her.

When I became a primary school teacher I assumed that the phonic method would work for everyone else just as well as it had worked for me. I was wrong. Every so often I read a newspaper article by some journalist who has taught her children to read the same way Nanna taught me. So she knows all about the teaching of reading and can't understand why the stupid teaching profession hasn't worked out what to do. I'd like to put these middle-class mothers – and politicians with the same opinion – in an inner city classroom and leave them there for a week or two. They would soon find out that it is more difficult than they think. Nanna's method doesn't work for everybody.

I was five or six when I dismissed Nanna and read the book to myself. After that I didn't let her read to me any more. I was a big girl, who read to herself. When I think about this now, I feel very sad, and wish we'd gone on sharing stories for longer.

My mother read to me too, usually at bedtime. *Black Beauty* was one of the books she read to me. But once I could read to myself, I put a stop to this as well.

I developed a reputation as a bookworm. My mother used to say, 'It's no good talking to her when she's got her head in a book. She can't hear you.' I think my family actually believed this. It wasn't true, but it was useful. If anybody tried to interrupt my reading, I pretended to be entirely unaware of them until they started shouting. Then I would look up innocently and say: 'Sorry, I didn't hear you.'

Along with food, reading was my comforter. I was glad to be able to escape from family life by retreating to my room with a book. I could enter a world that had nothing to do with any of them, and get to know some different people. If a book absorbed me, I hated getting to the end. I still do. I begin to slow down and ration myself because I don't want to say goodbye to that world and its characters.

Fortunately one doesn't always have to. Enid Blyton wrote series of books featuring the same people. I read all the Famous Five and the Secret Seven but my favourite was the Malory Towers series. Like J.K. Rowling with the Harry Potter books, Blyton takes her central character and friends through seven years of boarding school, one book for each year. The heroine is Darrell Rivers. After a few years she is joined at school by her younger sister, Felicity. I began reading these books before I went to boarding school, thereby acquiring the belief that it isn't done to cry or be homesick. When I finished the seventh and last book, I considered writing to the author and asking her to produce some more. Darrell had left school but Felicity was still there, so it seemed to me there was scope for a few more volumes. But I never got round to it.

As well as Enid Blyton I liked stories about dogs – *Greyfriars Bobby*, *Lassie Come Home* – and horses. My favourite horse books were the series by Ruby Ferguson that begins with *Jill's Gymkhana*. I had had some experience of riding a horse – a doctor recommended it for my knock knees when I was four or five. I learned to mount and dismount and rise to the trot but I never got as far as cantering or galloping. I loved it all – the ponies, the stable yard, the tackle. Regular riding lessons stopped after I went away to school. I read books about fortunate girls who had their own ponies, and asked my parents, from time to time, why we couldn't keep one in the back garden.

In some horse books the heroine also shows an interest in boys. For me this was a complete turn-off. What I wanted was a heroine who was entirely focused on the welfare of her pony, on learning skills, and on winning rosettes.

A worse turn-off was the horse story with a Christian

message. My mother occasionally tried to manipulate me into reading one of these, pretending it was an ordinary pony book. The first time I began reading one of these I was appalled when I realised what I had got myself into. After that I merely checked out the blurb. It always gave the game away.

Some of my reading was a bit more literary. My mother knew enough to put some children's classics my way – *Little Women* and *Good Wives*, *What Katy Did* and the rest of the series, *The Jungle Books*. I adored *The Jungle Books*, becoming deeply attached to Baloo the bear and Bagheera the panther. In *Don't Tell the Grown Ups*, her book about children's literature, Alison Lurie says that Kipling differs from most other popular children's authors. Whereas most of them are subversive, he is authoritarian. No wonder I liked him so much. A 'good' elder child, I have always tended to side with authority.

I hated the whole idea of the Disneyfication of *The Jungle Books*. I was an adult by the time the film was made and for many years refused to watch it. In the end I was persuaded it was really good, and sat down with the video. Well, the songs are enjoyable and the rest is OK, if you can manage to forget Kipling's original.

The Disneyfication of *Winnie-the-Pooh* depressed me even more. I've never seen the film but it is impossible to avoid noticing the spin-off products. I detest them.

The way children react to the Pooh books is very interesting. I was already familiar with them when I discovered, at the age of seven or eight, that they are really funny. Before that, I had quite enjoyed them as stories about animals in a wood. When I was a teacher

I read them to a class of nine- and ten-year-olds and found them responding on two different levels. A small group of the brighter children fell about laughing and thought the books were wonderful. The rest seemed to like the stories but didn't get the joke. 'Miss,' a girl asked me when the others had gone out, 'what *is* a woozle?'

Pooh is a good poet. It wasn't until I was a published poet myself that I fully appreciated the interaction between the poet Pooh and the poet Eeyore. Eeyore's attempt at a poem, in the last chapter of *The House at Pooh Corner*, is hilariously bad, though he evidently believes he has come up with a masterpiece. Pooh is touchingly willing to believe that Eeyore's poem is much better than his.

One of the problems Eeyore fails to solve is caused by the addition of an 's' to verbs in the third person singular. He rhymes 'friends' with 'send' and realises that won't work. Then he tries 'friend' and he finds he needs the verb 'sends'. He finds the business of writing a poem is more difficult than he had imagined.

I have noticed that some living poets solve Eeyore's problem by ignoring it. They just go right ahead and rhyme 'friend' with 'sends' or 'cat' with 'mats'. I suppose it makes things easier.

As a child, I wasn't excited about poetry, and rarely read any in my spare time. The poetry we did at school, as I have mentioned in an earlier chapter, was mainly about nature or fairies, and I didn't go for it.

My parents decided that I should have elocution lessons – an optional extra, like piano lessons. I hated the elocution lessons, and, by association, the poems I was made to elocute. The teacher decided to put me in for a competition. The set poem was 'Who Has Seen the Wind?' by Christina Rossetti. I was trained to recite it in a revoltingly dramatic way, with emphasis on extended vowels.

Whooo has seeen the wiiiind?
Neither yooooo nor Iiiii.

The competition was a disaster because it turned out that the poem has three stanzas. My teacher had used a book in which only two of them were printed. As I sat listening to the first competitor, my heart sank. The second entrant stepped up, and she, too, knew three stanzas. My teacher and my parents were there. They told me not to worry, it wasn't my fault. My teacher had a word with the judge and explained her mistake. When it was my turn the audience were told that I had only been taught the first two verses. I went up and recited them. Everyone was nice about it. My parents congratulated me, but I knew they must be upset on my behalf, and that upset me too. Obviously I had no chance of winning. And no chance at all of ever getting to like 'Who Has Seen the Wind?'

There was another one by Christina Rossetti that we did in the classroom. 'Margaret has a milking pail/ And she rises early . . .'. Frankly, my dears, as Molesworth would say, I couldn't have cared less whether Margaret had a milking pail, a pet elephant, or double pneumonia. Later on in life I gave Christina Rossetti another chance and discovered she wrote some wonderful poems about love and death. We didn't do love and death at Ashford Junior School.

At home I was subjected to different poetry. My father liked to recite favourites he knew by heart. We didn't encourage him to give us 'The Charge of the Light Brigade' or stanzas from *The Rubaiyat of Omar Khayyam* over lunch. But, if the mood took him, we got it anyway. The poems he made us listen to are now among my favourites too. It's odd how it can go either way. Junior school put me off all sorts of things, including, I am sad to say, *A Midsummer Night's Dream*. Bored to distraction by my early experience of church, I have grown up to love *The Book of Common Prayer* and the hymns we sang.

There is one important omission from this account of my early reading: Nigel Molesworth. More of him later.

Unpublished memoir

My Book of the Century
Wendy Cope makes her choice

Quite frankly my deres i do not kno what is the grate book of the century becos there are 1 or 2 famous ones i hav not read yet. But keen literrary editor twist my arm chiz saing it is not THE book of the century it is A book eg anething you like reelly. O go on pleez it would be wonderful to hav contribution from you. Do i hav to flater you for half an hour or will this be enuff?

i scratch head in deep thort. altho i do not litely dismiss the clames of s freud v woolf t s eliot wittgenstein or j derrida (and i will tuough you up if you sugest i hav not the fanetest clue about eny of them) i chuse rather to sing the praises of *Down with Skool!* (1953) cheers cheers cheers and its immortal hero and narator nigel molesworth the curse of st custard's.

Molesworth cast a cynical eye over his skool (built by a madman in 1836) and the oiks wets and weeds who attend it. we meet his frend peason, his bro molesworth 2 ('it panes me to think i am of the same blud') and fotherington-tomas who go round saing hullo clouds hullo sky and blub in eng lessons becos the master read peoms so beatifully.

Our hero hav little time for peotry ('sissy stuff that rhymes') or for any academick pursute tho his comments on the arts ('Personally it is not the noise i object to in music, it is the words') are sometimes spot on.

i hav been reading this stuff and roaring with larffter since i was 11 yrs old which some people would sa explane a lot. hav molesworth influenced me or do i enjoy it becos i was like that in the first place? I cannot sa. But I would contend hem hem that geoffrey willans author of *Down with Skool!* and sequles was one of the outstanding humuorists of our century and deserv to be much more famous. The piktures (r searle) are v funny too.

A cupple of weeks ago i learn that all molesworth books are currantly out of print chiz chiz chiz. it go to show that publishers are uterly wet and weedy bunch of cissies greedy guts and oiks. i diskard them.

Daily Telegraph 1999

Molesworth

In 1956, when I was eleven years old, my mother took my sister and me to a book exhibition in London. She told us we could choose one book each. My eye fell on a volume entitled *Down with Skool!* I picked it up, looked at the opening pages, and was captivated.

'This is the book I want,' I said.

'Are you sure, darling? It looks like a boys' book.'

I was sure, so she bought it for me. Back home, I read it that evening, crying with laughter. I have been captivated ever since.

Down with Skool! was first published in 1953 by Max Parrish and Co. Ltd, of Queen Anne Street, London W1. More than 50,000 copies were sold within a year and, by the time I acquired a copy in 1956, it had been reprinted six times. Unfortunately the dust jacket has gone missing, so I don't know how much my mother paid for it. The second Molesworth book, *How to be Topp*, appeared in 1954 but my copy is a Puffin paperback, published in 1962 and reprinted in 1963. It cost three shillings. Why did I wait so long to buy it? I had seen it in a bookshop and found that the first few pages were exactly the same as the opening pages of *Down with Skool!* I concluded that this was the same book with a different title and only found out a long time afterwards that I was wrong. Presumably the publishers thought that St Custard's and its leading characters needed to be introduced again for the benefit of new readers. In complete editions of Molesworth the overlap has been removed.

Whizz for Atomms appeared in 1956 and was reprinted the same year. My copy is from the second impression. The price has been cut off the dust jacket (it must have been a present) but the back flap offers the two earlier volumes at 9s 6d each. In 1959 I invested 10s 6d in a copy of *Back in the Jug Agane* as soon as it came out. I am the proud owner of a first edition, first printing, with a badly torn dust jacket. A compendium edition, *The Compleet Molesworth*, appeared at around the same time as the fourth volume.

By the time these last two books were published, their author, Geoffrey Willans, was dead. This sad fact is not mentioned on the dust jacket and I didn't learn it until many years later. Though his books are famous, Willans was and is less well known and less celebrated than he deserves to be. There is, now, an entry in the *Oxford Dictionary of National Biography*, but only since 2004. It says that he was born on 4 February 1911 in England. Willans's nephew, Robin Gilbert, tells me that his uncle was, in fact, born in Smyrna (now Izmir in Turkey), where his father, George Herbert Willans, was Assistant Locomotive, Carriage and Wagon Superintendent of the Ottoman Aidan Railway. Geoffrey was educated at Glyngarth Preparatory School in Gloucestershire, and then at Blundell's School, Tiverton. After leaving school he taught at Woodcote House, a Surrey prep school. According to Robin Gilbert, there is some evidence that he also taught at Carn Brea School in Bromley. Ronald Searle, who was a friend before they worked together on Molesworth, has expressed the opinion that Willans 'must have been a jolly nice schoolmaster'.

The rest of Searle's description is worth quoting. According to him, Willans was 'shortish, dapper – a careful dresser. Very accessible, with a splendid broad smile. Slightly clownlike . . . But there was nothing clownish about him. Entirely professional. Friendly but not a dupe.'

After two or three years as a schoolmaster, Willans gave up teaching and became a freelance writer, contributing articles to *Punch* and other magazines. His first novel, *Shallow Dive*, appeared in 1934 and a second, *Romantic Manner*, in 1936. In 1940 he married Pamela Wyndham Gibbes. During the war he served as a temporary commissioned officer in the Royal Naval Volunteer Reserve, and wrote a book about his experiences (*One Eye on the Clock*, 1943). From 1945 until 1958 he was employed by the BBC in its European Service. The job did not prevent him from continuing to write articles and books.

Molesworth made his debut in some articles that Willans wrote for *Punch* between 1939 and 1942. Nowhere near as good as the books, these articles are instructive reading for a writer. They show just how much improvement can be brought about as a result of time, thought and revision. They also show how important Ronald Searle's contribution was to the finished product

– he didn't illustrate the *Punch* pieces. In 1952 Willans told Searle about his plan to write 'a full-length humorous book with a prep. school theme' and the successful collaboration began. It produced not only the Molesworth tetralogy but also *The Dog's Ear Book* (1958), an amusing concoction about dogs and their owners. Willans's other post-war publications included the novels *Crisis Cottage* (1956) and *Admiral on Horseback* (1954), both still readable. There is an account of a cricket match in the former that deserves to be anthologised. *Fasten Your Lapstraps!* (1955), a humorous book about being an airline passenger, is interesting as social history. *My Uncle Harry* (1957), a fictional portrait of an eccentric gentleman, has less to offer the twenty-first-century reader. Willans was also responsible for a biography of Peter Ustinov (*Peter Ustinov*, 1957) and co-wrote the screenplay for a film, *The Bridal Path*, which was released in 1959. On 6 August 1958 Willans died, of a heart attack, at the age of forty-seven.

The life and career of Ronald Searle are better known, so I will deal with them more briefly. Readers who want to know more can consult Russell Davies's biography, published in 1990 and still available. Born in 1920 in Cambridge, Searle became a cartoonist for a local newspaper at the age of fifteen. In 1939 he enlisted in the Territorial Army and in 1941 was posted to Singapore. When Singapore fell to the Japanese, he was taken prisoner, first in the prison camp at Changi, and then as a slave labourer on the Burma–Siam Railway. Searle's wartime drawings, published in *The Naked Island* in 1945, record what he saw around him – brutality, hunger, disease. After the war he achieved considerable success with his depictions of the girls of St Trinian's, which appeared in the magazine *Lilliput* and subsequently in book form. Then came Molesworth, and a distinguished career as a cartoonist, illustrator and painter. He has lived in France since 1961 and in 2004 was made a CBE.

The Molesworth books have been described as 'classics of humour in the English language'. In a recent radio programme, Tim Rice said they stood comparison 'with any funny book written in the last fifty or a hundred years'. After careful reflection I can honestly say that they are the funniest books I have ever read. Every time I reread them I come across something I'd forgotten that makes me laugh out loud. Most recently it was Grimes the headmaster explaining to a parent why music lessons will 'cost you ten nicker and not a penny less': 'Look at the wear and tear on the piano – it's a bektenstein, you kno. Then there's the metronome – had to have new sparking plugs last hols.'

Molesworth's views on Grimes, the other masters, his fellow pupils, parents, education and, indeed, on life, are utterly cynical. For me, an eleven-year-old reader of girls' school fiction, he was a wonderful antidote to the relentlessly positive attitudes in those books, and to the pieties expressed by adults and the media in the 1950s. 'Who knows what adventures in work and pla the new term will bring forth. And who cares, eh?'

There are dozens of favourite passages I would like to quote. In view of the direction my life has taken, the number one slot goes to Molesworth on the art he usually calls 'peotry'. 'Peotry is sissy stuff that rhymes. Weedy people say la and fie and swoon when they see a bunch of daffodils.' He gives us an unforgettable portrait of a poetry-lover: 'And who is this who skip weedily up to me, eh? "Hullo clouds, hullo sky, he sa. Hullo birds, hullo poetry books, hullo skool sossages, hullo molesworth 1." You hav guessed it is dere little basil fotherington-tomas.' It is salutary for a poet to be aware of Fotherington-Thomas. When I notice myself sounding like him, I try again.

Needless to say, my spellchecker has been going berserk while I copied out the quotations. Molesworth's spelling is beautifully judged. He makes just the right proportion of errors, and then surprises us with the correct spelling of words such as 'temporarily' or 'discovered'. His grammar and syntax are even more important – an essential element of that engaging and memorable voice. Once you've got into Molesworth, it is difficult not to talk like him. My conversation is peppered with his expressions – 'as any fule kno', 'chiz chiz', 'curses wot am i saing?', 'I will tuough him up' (pronounced too oaf), 'hem hem' – and with the habitual use of 'hav' instead of 'has' – as in 'History started badly and hav been getting steadily worse'. I try not to do it in the company of people who may not be *aficionados* (hem hem) but recognition of Molesworth-speak is pleasingly widespread. Now and again, 'as any fule kno' pops up in the middle of an article, without any explanation. That is as it should be.

The pictures are just as memorable. No Molesworth fan can hear mention of the Gauls or the Romans without seeing Searle's portraits of *A Gaul marching into Italy* and *A Roman marching into Gaul* and remembering their wonderful irrelevance to the text that surrounds them. I am particularly fond of *The Private Life of the Gerund*. When I first came across it, I had never heard of a gerund. Later on, in Latin lessons, I learned and forgot what it was, but I still know what it looks like. Yet Searle's greatest triumphs in these books are his portrayals of the boys and the masters. Molesworth's face is exactly as it should be – the intelligence, the aggression, the refusal to be impressed. The series of drawings entitled *Masters at a Glance* is still popular with teachers. 'I am still hoping for a job in the colonial service somewhere' may be outdated but 'No. The spirit of tolerance, you fool' and 'Of course the fellow doesn't realise he's a typical schoolmaster' are right on the button to this day.

In his excellent article on Molesworth published in the *Independent* in 1992, Kevin Jackson says that Searle's cartoons are linked to Willans's text 'as indissolubly as Tenniel's drawings are to Lewis Carroll's'. I used to think that E.H. Shepard's illustrations were indissolubly linked to A.A. Milne's Pooh stories. Let us hope that the Disney Corporation never gets its hands on Molesworth.

It is now more than fifty years since the publication of *Down with Skool!* Has Molesworth stood the test of time? Some commentators have suggested that the books are set in a world that is no longer recognisable, and that they have no relevance in the twenty-first century. In answer to that I would say that human nature hasn't changed very much since 1953. Human beings – their hopes and fears and aspirations, their pretensions and hypocrisies – are portrayed in these books with a perceptive brilliance that is unlikely ever to go out of date.

It's true that there are some references that may puzzle younger readers. Who was Gilbert Harding? You wouldn't have to be a genius to work out from the context that he appeared on television. Who were Stalin and Khrushchev? I am happy to say I have met young people who know the answer to that one. It's true that schoolmasters don't use canes any more but everyone knows they used to. I recently gave a copy of the Penguin edition to a young man who was born in the late 1980s. 'It's extremely funny,' he wrote. 'He really understands boys and the way they think.'

Some readers are uncomfortable about Molesworth's attitude to working-class boys, 'the oiks'. These books, they feel, are set in a class-ridden society and are unsuitable for us, now that we have moved on. Anyone who has heard middle-class teenagers talking about 'chavs' and 'townies' may take the view that we haven't moved on very far. The teenagers I have in mind were pupils at a comprehensive school. It wouldn't hurt us to read about a class-ridden society, even if we didn't still live in one, but, as it happens, we do.

For the last thirteen years I have lived with a man who teaches in an independent school for boys. It is a boarding school and I am part of the community. This experience has refreshed my enjoyment of Molesworth. Walking past the playing fields, I spot a master who 'think he can score a gole with his own voice'. He may not actually be yelling 'COME ON ST CUSTARD'S . . . GET INTO HIM . . . PASS! . . . MARK YORE MAN!'

but it is something very like it. I had better not go so far as to say that Sigismund the mad maths master is alive and well, but I will mention that maths departments are not noted for their sanity. When the school assembles, under the watchful eyes of the headmaster and his deputy, it is impossible not to think of Grimes turning to G.A. Postlethwaite and asking him: 'Are they all in, Slugsy?'

In his 'Prefface' to *Whizz for Atomms*, Molesworth includes some acknowledgements. 'My thanks are due to grabber for the use of his blotch, peason whose pen I pinched and the skool gardener for cleaning out the ink wells – a task which only a man with iron nerve can perform. I gratefully acknowledge the kindly help and encouragement of gillibrand, a most lively source of material ha-ha the dere little wet. molesworth 2 was just about able to read the proofs and pass the spelling.' My thanks (more sincere and less qualified than Molesworth's) are due to Robin Gilbert for his invaluable help, to John Thorn, to Lachlan Mackinnon, and to his father, another Lachlan Mackinnon, who read the typescript and passed the spelling.

Introduction to the Folio Society edition of 'The Compleet Molesworth' 2007

Anne Sexton

Anne Sexton: A Biography by Diane Wood Middlebrook
Selected Poems of Anne Sexton eds. Diane Wood
Middlebrook and Diana Hume George

'Even crazy, I'm as nice as a chocolate bar,' wrote Anne
Sexton, in a poem called 'Live'. Crazy she certainly was,
but few readers of Diane Wood Middlebrook's fascinating
biography will go along with the other adjective in that
quotation.

Born in 1928, Sexton was the daughter of an affluent
Boston wool merchant. Mental illness ran in the family.
Her paternal grandfather had a breakdown, and a great
aunt went mad. Her father was an alcoholic. In the years
following Anne's suicide in 1974, two other relations
also took their own lives.

Anne married at twenty, and first tried to kill herself
after the birth of her second daughter. She entered psychotherapy with Dr Martin Orne, a key figure in her life
story. It was Dr Orne who suggested that 'she begin
writing about her experiences in order to help other
patients'. His idea proved astonishingly fruitful. Sexton
wrote, attended workshops, made friends with other
poets. Within four years she had published a well-received

book. In 1967 she was awarded the Pulitzer Prize for her third collection, *Live or Die*. She also won readers – by poetry standards her books sold unusually well – and the affections of a series of lovers.

Meanwhile her husband, Kayo Sexton, who had been obliged to give up his own dream of becoming a doctor, continued to support his wife and children by working as a salesman. Since Anne refused to let anything get in the way of her writing, he usually shopped for food and cooked the evening meal.

'Sexton caused her family great distress,' says Middlebrook, 'by insisting on the primacy, at all times, of her needs, and this did not change. Sometimes these were needs for care, sometimes for allowances; she wanted to be able to ignore the family at will.' Ignoring the family was not the worst of it – Sexton's elder daughter, Linda, told Middlebrook she had been sexually abused by her mother.

Though Anne and Kayo had violent fights, she dreaded his absence on business trips. She hated to be alone. Despite this dependence, she decided in 1973 that she wanted a divorce. The children were by now away at boarding school and college. Without the underpinning provided by her family, Sexton went to pieces, relying more and more on pills and alcohol, and exhausting the goodwill of friends. On 4 October 1974, she got into her car, in a closed garage, and switched on the ignition.

My intense antipathy to the subject of this biography undoubtedly owes something to the fact that I am a woman poet who has lived alone and paid my own way. It does not seem to be shared by Diane Wood Middlebrook, an impressive author, who does her best to be fair to everyone involved. She pronounces judgement only when it is unavoidable, as in the case of Sexton's second psychotherapist, who had an affair with his patient.

The first psychotherapist, Dr Orne, comes close to being the hero of the book. Had he not moved away to Philadelphia in 1964, the poet might be alive today. He is now at the centre of a controversy because he allowed her biographer to listen to tapes of his sessions with Sexton, a decision he defends in a foreword on the grounds that his patient would not have minded.

I agree with those who consider the decision unethical. The point is not what Sexton would have wanted, but the effect on other patients, who need to have faith in the confidentiality of the consulting room. At the same time it cannot be denied that Middlebrook's access to the tapes has enhanced the readability of her book.

It is utterly compelling, not just as the story of one woman's life, but also as a picture of the American literary scene in the Sixties and Seventies, with glimpses of such figures as Robert Lowell and Sylvia Plath.

One thing Middlebrook does not tell us is what has happened to Sexton's reputation in the United States since her death. On this side of the Atlantic her stock has fallen very low, and she has been omitted from several important anthologies. Having read two of her late collections in the Seventies, and made little of them, I did not expect much from Virago's new *Selected Poems of Anne Sexton*.

It was an agreeable surprise to find, in the first half of the book, many well-made and accessible poems.

Sexton was often at her best when writing about other people – her beloved great aunt, her daughter ('small piglet, butterfly/ girl with jelly bean cheeks,/ disobedient three, my splendid/ stranger'), or an unknown girl in a maternity ward.

Her poems about herself are harder to take. In one of them, 'In Celebration of My Uterus', she carries on like a female Fotherington-Thomas: 'Hello spirit. Hello, cup.' Much of her later work reads like chopped-up prose, and the self-dramatising tone often becomes monotonous. It is easy to see why some people dismiss Anne Sexton. But it is the good poems that matter in the long run, and there are good poems here.

Daily Telegraph 1991

Christina Rossetti

*Learning Not to be First: A Life of Christina Rossetti
by Kathleen Jones*

Biographies of women poets seldom make cheerful reading. With Christina Rossetti, at least one knows that the story does not end in suicide. All the same, it is a sad one.

Born in London in 1830 to an Italian father and a half-Italian mother, Christina was a vivacious, open child, 'given to terrible tantrums'. In the family, she and her brother Dante Gabriel were known as 'the two storms'. In adolescence she underwent a metamorphosis, painfully taming her own nature to conform to a very strict interpretation of Christianity. As an adult she was 'shy, over-restrained, over-scrupulous'. Kathleen Jones calls this process 'social and emotional maiming'.

When love came along, she turned it away on religious grounds. Her first suitor, the painter James Collinson, was, by all accounts, one of the less impressive members of the Pre-Raphaelite Brotherhood. He had been converted to Catholicism. Christina, like her mother, was an Anglican. It seems that she loved him, but she felt she must refuse his proposal of marriage.

Collinson rethought his conversion, rejoined the Anglican Communion, and was accepted. Two years later he changed his mind again, and reverted to the Church of Rome. Christina broke off the engagement. Subsequently she wrote heart-rending poems about the agony of relinquishing love.

One does not have to look very far to observe that weak and unexceptional people can inspire intense romantic feeling. None the less, some of Christina's biographers have found it difficult to believe that her early love poems can really be about Collinson. L.M. Packer argued that she was secretly in love with a married man, William Bell Scott. Kathleen Jones disagrees, and presents evidence that makes this affair seem unlikely.

Still, there are lines that puzzle:

None know the choice I made; I make it still.
None know the choice I made and broke my heart.

The engagement to Collinson was not secret, nor was its severance. It is difficult to dismiss the possibility that there was more to all this than biographers have been able to dig up.

As Jones points out, Christina is not an easy subject. She confided little to those around her. Much of the documentary evidence – letters and journal entries – was destroyed by the poet or by friends and relatives at her request. Inevitably, this biography stimulates as much curiosity as it satisfies.

One of the strengths of the book is the way Kathleen Jones maps the links between Christina and other women poets of her time. She shows that the four major figures – Rossetti, Elizabeth Barrett Browning, Emily Brontë and Emily Dickinson – although they never met, 'read each other's work and influenced each other more than has been previously acknowledged'.

Victorian women, if they wrote poetry, were expected to write about the beauties of nature. A letter survives in which Dante Gabriel urges Christina to do just that. But all four of these women transcended such expectations: 'The passionate internal "dreamings" of Brontë, Dickinson and Rossetti, the polemics of Barrett Browning, were something entirely new.'

Looking at their lives, Jones notes some interesting parallels. Illness played a useful role for at least three of them, leaving the young Elizabeth Barrett 'free from irksome domestic and social duties', and making it impossible for Emily Brontë or Christina to take teaching jobs away from home.

In Christina's case the brave, passionate dreamer continued to be a rigid puritan. She gave up playing chess because she enjoyed winning. She pasted strips of paper over the lines in Swinburne's poems that offended her. She had no time for the work of George Eliot because she disapproved of that author's morals.

In her late thirties she turned down a second suitor, Charles Cayley, because he was an agnostic. She certainly loved Cayley, and the decision was painful. Like the earlier renunciation, it gave rise to powerful poems. Her 'Monna Innominata' sequence, written at this time, ends with the almost unbearably bleak sonnet, 'Youth gone, and beauty gone'.

From 1870 onwards much of Christina's energy was spent on caring for others – her elderly mother, her aunts, the dying Dante Gabriel. Published, recognised, she grew more and more diffident. Towards the end of her life she was tormented by guilt about past sins and misdemeanours. She died of cancer in 1894.

Daily Telegraph 1991

Office Life

The Chatto Book of Office Life:
Or Love Among the Filing Cabinets
ed. Jeremy Lewis

I am a self-employed writer. Some days I stay home and do very little work. Other days I go out and do not do any. When my guilt and anxiety about this become oppressive, I think back to the two and a half years I spent 'working' in an office. Taking into account the lunch breaks, the pauses for conversation, the point-less meetings, and time spent raging at an inoperative photocopier, how many hours of productive activity did my colleagues and I squeeze into a day? It cannot have been any more than I manage now.

Jeremy Lewis, editor of *The Chatto Book of Office Life*, confirms this comforting belief: 'More often than not, it [work] takes up only a modest proportion of the eight hours or so that are devoted to it,' he says in his introduction to a section called 'Getting Down to Work'. The first item in the section, an excerpt from *Psmith in the City* by P.G. Wodehouse, bears the title 'Nothing to Do Until Lunch'. The second is from Pepys's Diary: '13th January 1660. To my office, where nothing to do. 14th January. Nothing to do at our office . . .'

Now and again the reader of this anthology will catch a glimpse of someone filing, making an entry in a ledger, dictating or typing letters, or sticking stamps on them. The hardest workers in the book are the clerks in Herman Melville's *Bartleby*, copying documents by hand, and the bond salesmen in Tom Wolfe's *The Bonfire of the Vanities*, on the telephone all day in an office where only the boldest of rebels dares read a newspaper.

Early in his own office career, Jeremy Lewis was rebuked for reading *Nicholas Nickleby* at his desk. His offence was not failure to work but failure to pay attention to a game of office cricket his colleagues were playing with rulers and a ball of crumpled paper. Office cricket comes under 'Ritual, Gossip and the Social Whirl'. Other sections deal with 'The Interview', 'Office Politics', 'Eating Lunch', 'Office Parties', and, of course, 'Love Among the Filing Cabinets'.

In his introduction, the editor warns us not to expect a history of the office, or advice about 'where to place one's desk in order to gain a psychological advantage'. 'What interests me,' he continues, 'are the reactions of articulate but pleasingly run-of-the-mill nine-to-fivers.'

He found that few modern novelists have written well about his chosen topic. Those who have turn up over and over again – there are twelve excerpts from the novels by Roy Fuller, eight from *Office Life* by Keith Waterhouse, five from Nicholson Baker's *The Mezzanine*. Two earlier authors achieve an even higher score – there are twenty entries by Dickens and twenty-two by Sinclair Lewis.

The result is an enjoyable patchwork, in which the reader meets the same author, and the same characters, more often than is usual in a thematic anthology. This makes it more suitable than most for reading from cover to cover, rather than dipping in at random.

Most readers will not mind that the editor has included only a small ration of poetry. Office life has not inspired a lot of verse, though it proved a fruitful subject for Gavin Ewart, who has three poems in the book, as does Sir John Betjeman. I was sorry not to find the Ewart poem that begins 'In the long and boring meeting . . .' And it is a pity that no one pointed Jeremy Lewis in the direction of *Selected Poems* by Carol Rumens, also published by Chatto. Her 'Gifts and Loans', describing a friendship that has grown into contented, unspoken love, is the most beautiful office poem I know.

A poem like that would have done something to lift the prevailing tone of the book. But perhaps it is inevitable that an anthology on this subject should, despite a wealth of humorous contributions, leave one reflecting on the sadness and futility of life. The most melancholy chapter is the last one, 'The End of the Road', in which a series of characters go through the retirement ritual – the gathering, the farewell speech, the presentation of a clock.

'I was in the condition of a prisoner in the old Bastile [sic], suddenly let loose after forty years' confinement,' wrote Charles Lamb in his essay 'The Superannuated Man'. 'I missed my chains.' But Lamb offers some hope to those approaching retirement. Within a few weeks he had adjusted to his new freedom, and felt pretty much the way one feels when writing the last sentence of a book review: 'I have worked task work, and have the rest of the day to myself.'

Daily Telegraph 1992

Gavin Ewart
Gavin Ewart: Selected
Poems 1933–1993

'So the last date slides into the bracket,' wrote Gavin
Ewart in his memorial poem to Sir John Betjeman (1906–
84). Eleven years later the last date slid into Gavin's own
bracket. This selection was made by the poet himself
before he died in October 1995, aged seventy-nine.

A *Selected Poems* from this author was long overdue.
Ewart wrote a lot and published most of it, even though
he was well aware that, as he once said to me: 'Some
of them are only so-so.' 'If I leave something out,' he
explained, 'someone always complains that it was their
favourite.'

This policy was generous to his readers, but it did
not do much for his literary reputation. Ewart was philo-
sophical about reputation. In a sonnet called 'Afterwards',
he wryly summed up what he expected of posterity:
'They'll say (if I'm lucky):/ He wrote some silly poems,
and some of them were funny.' Sure enough, one reviewer
of this book has opined that the poet has achieved as
much eminence 'as could reasonably be due to an art so
free of seriousness'.

This verdict is incomprehensible. Take, for example, 'The Daytime Mugging in the High Street'. The first thirteen lines describe an attack on an old lady, pushed into the road by a youth who was after her purse: 'All the conventional judgments/ say what a terrible thing (true) and what a terrible man!'

In the fourteenth and last line comes the surprise: 'But I say, too, she *might* still be better off than a tormented young junkie.' That is a serious poem about a contemporary issue, if ever there was one.

War, usually reckoned to be the kind of thing serious poets write about, is the subject of several of Ewart's poems. Some of them draw on his memories of active service in the Second World War. Later, he wrote about the Falklands, and at the time of the Gulf War composed 'The War Song of Lewis Carroll', which begins:

> *I saw my little son without his head,*
> *I saw the tortured and I saw the dead –*
> *'Why, this is most peculiar!' I said.*

It is very different from Wilfred Owen, but it is a powerful response to the horror of war.

In 'The Moment' Ewart likens the first appearance of enemy troops to the first recognition, by old people, of 'the unambiguous symptoms'. Death is as pervasive in Ewart as it is in the work of Philip Larkin. Like Larkin, he believed that 'we're certainly faced with oblivion'. Unlike Larkin, he said so in a limerick.

One of the differences between these two poets is that in the work of Gavin Ewart we also find love

– for his wife and family, and for his friends. His poems about loved ones often have a poignancy that moves the reader to tears. As another poet once said to me: 'When Gavin isn't making you laugh, he's making you cry.'

'Is my emotion bogus or inflationary?' he asks at one point. It is a question every poet needs to ask continually, and Ewart was too good ever to forget it. He eschewed heightened language, writing with a simplicity that can sometimes mislead the reader into thinking that the poet is merely stating the obvious. There is a double-take effect, as you realise that it was not obvious until you read the poem.

The ability to say things simply was coupled with high technical skill, especially in the handling of metre. There is tremendous formal variety in this book, and linguistic variety too – two or three poems in Scots, one in Latin, one in Franglais. The breadth of Ewart's learning is evident in poems about Gibbon, Pepys, the city of Pompeii, the Battle of Agincourt, as well as in several (not my favourites) displaying an encyclopedic knowledge of cricket. Those, like Gavin's much celebrated bawdy poems, are more popular with men.

His unfailing ability to spot the bogus or inflationary in others provided material for many of his humorous poems. It is as if the child in the story of the Emperor's new clothes had grown up without losing his clearsightedness, his refusal to be deflected from telling the truth. Ewart did not ignore literary fashion: he laughed at it. He laughed at the posturing of poets, at the critics, and at idiocy, especially solemn idiocy, wherever he found it.

He was a wise, compassionate and serious poet who could be gloriously funny. Read him. He will help to keep you sane.

Daily Telegraph 1996

This book is now published by the print-on-demand series Faber Finds (see the Faber & Faber website). Second-hand copies and ebook editions are available.

Larkin's 'First Sight'

When I first read Philip Larkin's 'First Sight', it knocked me sideways. It made me cry. I was amazed and grateful and sad and happy, all at the same time. I read it again, and sat and thought about it for a while. I didn't want to go straight on and read something else. It's a good feeling, when a poem gets to you like that.

'First Sight' is not the only poem in the English language to have had this effect on me. It's not unusual for me to be asked to name a favourite poem and I am on record – in various charity anthologies – as having several different ones. This poem is one of my special favourites, and has been for a quarter of a century.

There's a personal reason why it moves me so much. I suffered from depression for many years and, by chance, I came across the poem at a time when the sun was just beginning to come out in my life. But I wouldn't have responded in the way I did if the poem hadn't been so well crafted.

Larkin devotes more than half the fourteen lines (the poem is an unconventional sonnet) to the 'vast unwelcome' of a cold winter. It isn't until line 10 that there is a hint of something better to come. And then, suddenly, he hits us with the magnificent line 'Earth's immeasurable surprise', leading on to that wonderful final couplet. He doesn't mention sunshine or daffodils or green grass – he doesn't need to. By the time we reach the end of the poem, we are imagining the spring.

Waterstones' Magazine 2001

Philip Larkin

I have been feeling very sad about Larkin. I did a reading on Monday evening and would have liked to begin it with a favourite Larkin poem. But when I looked at them in the afternoon I found that they all made me cry.

You will have seen the picture in today's *Observer* and the caption. 'PHILIP LARKIN: What will survive of us is love.' Almost right. What will survive of us will be quoted out of context.

Letter to D.M. Thomas 1985

Terry Street
by Douglas Dunn

Terry Street was first published in 1969, but I wasn't much of a poetry reader at the time and didn't come across it until a few years later. My interest in reading and writing poems began late in 1972. In a random and unguided way, I set about discovering what poets were doing nowadays.

At the time, I was teaching in a primary school just off the Old Kent Road in south London. When I first went there the school was surrounded by streets of old terraced houses. They were scheduled for demolition, to make way for Burgess Park. By the time I left the school in 1981 most of the houses had disappeared and the residents had been moved into horrible estates like the notorious Aylesbury. When I chanced upon a copy of *Terry Street*, perhaps in 1973 or 1974, the houses were still there and the setting of Dunn's poems was very recognisable.

I found the book absorbing. Here was a poet who was writing about the kind of place I was working in, the kind of people I was working with. He helped to dispel my vague notion that poets had to live somewhere beautiful and write about nature. I did know that he wasn't the first poet to bring the city into his poems – I had read some Eliot. But I hadn't come across anything like this – an affectionate, observant account of life in a working-class city street, written by someone who actually lived there.

My favourite poem in the book was and still is 'A Removal from Terry Street', better known, perhaps, as 'the one with the lawnmower'. Mention *Terry Street* to just about anyone who reads poetry and they will quote the last line: 'That man, I wish him well. I wish him grass.' Every time I read that it gives me goose pimples and brings tears to my eyes. It wouldn't, of course, work so well if the preceding lines were not so perfect – the description of the family with their 'squeaking cart', their 'cups, carpets, chairs,/ Four paperback westerns.' And the lawnmower. And then 'There is no grass in Terry Street. The worms/ Come up cracks in concrete yards in moonlight.'

Dunn doesn't prettify the street. He describes the litter, 'fag-packets,/ Balls of fish and chip newspaper', and is particularly good on city sounds, 'the ticking of bicycle chains,/ Sudden blasts of motorcycles, whimpering of vans.' I was struck by the way he finds beautiful, lyrical moments among all these unbeautiful details – when, for example, the men of Terry Street 'hold up their children and sing to them' or the builder's trowel 'catches the light and becomes precious'. And I found the poet's persona engaging. 'A Dream of Judgement' (in the second, non-*Terry Street* section) is addressed to Samuel Johnson. 'Licking your boots is a small Scotsman/ Who looks like Boswell, but is really me.' You can't help but like the poet who wrote that.

How much of the world of *Terry Street* would be familiar to a young person now? Young women in 'teasing skirts and latest shoes,/ Lush, impermanent coats' can still be seen on any street but they probably don't have old-fashioned sewing machines at home. Fewer old men wear long underwear or take their laundry to the Bendix or have 'pocket watches/ Muffled under ancient overcoats'. Some google research reveals that the terraced houses of Terry Street have been replaced by modern ones, which sell for well under £100,000. Dunn's book is now an interesting slice of social history, as well as a brilliant collection of poems.

Did *Terry Street* influence me? I hate being asked about influences. In a recent interview the American novelist Shalom Auslander responded thus to a question about literary influences: 'I have no idea – I know who I like, I know who inspires me . . . but whether they influence my writing or not is for others to decide.' Exactly. *Terry Street* continues to inspire me, as does some of Douglas Dunn's later work. 'The Year's Afternoon' is one of my favourite poems of all time. I suspect that his influence is detectable in the early poems I wrote about the children I was teaching and their environment. Those poems never made it into print – they are juvenilia. However, working on them was a valuable part of the learning process. If I hadn't read *Terry Street*, I might not have attempted them.

The Dark Horse 2012

George Herbert

Like many other people, I first came across the work of George Herbert very early in life. In church and the school chapel I sang the hymns 'Teach Me, My God and King', 'King of Glory, King of Peace' and 'Let All the World in Ev'ry Corner Sing' without taking any notice of the name of the person who wrote the words. Many years later, as an adult who had developed an interest in poetry, I bought a selection of Herbert's poems in a second-hand bookshop. I was pleasantly surprised to find that I already knew some of them almost by heart.

As I had never done Herbert in English lessons at school, most of his work was new to me. I took to it immediately. What especially appealed to me – and still does – was this poet's wonderfully playful delight in poetic form, and the fact that his poems are, at the same time, utterly serious. All of them (except some of the Latin poems he wrote in his youth) are on religious themes. In our time there is a tendency to associate technical bravura with 'light verse'. Herbert is one of the poets who shows us that this need not be so. There is humour, as well as exuberant inventiveness, in his work, but no one challenges his standing as a serious poet, whose primary concern was not to show off but to tell the truth.

When I first read that second-hand book, I was not a churchgoer and thought of myself as an atheist. Over the years, critics have discussed whether or not one needs to be a believing Christian to appreciate Herbert's poems. I can answer this question with confidence: one does not. I should add, however, that my upbringing and education were Christian. Had they not been, I would have found Herbert harder to understand. In the past nine years, since I began going to church again, I have grown still fonder of these poems, valuing them, to borrow a phrase from Auden, as 'expressions of Anglican piety at its best'.

Herbert was born in Montgomery in 1593, twenty-nine years after the birth of Shakespeare and ten years before the death of Queen Elizabeth I. He was the seventh of ten children. His father, Richard Herbert (a descendant of the earls of Pembroke), died when George was three, leaving his mother, Magdalene, to bring up seven boys and three girls on her own. By all accounts she was a remarkable woman – strong, well educated and devoutly religious – and an important influence on George. The family moved to Oxford, and then to London, where he went to Westminster School. In 1609 Magdalene got married again, to a much younger man, Sir John Danvers. This seems to have caused some problems with Edward, the eldest of her offspring, but not with the younger children. Herbert's letters to Danvers are affectionate and respectful, and there is no evidence of hostility between them. In the reign of Charles I, Danvers was to be one of the regicides, signatories to the king's death warrant, but by then his stepson George was dead.

Herbert was a hard-working and successful schoolboy and, in the same year that his mother remarried, he was admitted to Trinity College, Cambridge. Here, too, he did well. By 1616 he was an MA and a major fellow of the college. In 1619 he was appointed to the prestigious post of public orator of Cambridge. He described his duties in a letter to his stepfather: '[The orator] writes all the University Letters, makes all the Orations, be it to King, Prince or whatever comes to the University.' He met King James I and got to know powerful courtiers. Herbert now had good prospects of achieving high public office, if he so wished.

At this point in the story there is some disagreement between modern scholars and Herbert's first biographer, Izaak Walton, whose *The Life of Mr George Herbert* was first published in 1670.

According to Walton, it was as a result of the deaths of his two most important patrons that a disappointed Herbert decided to 'enter into Sacred Orders'.

The truth, it seems, is not so simple. The biographer Amy Charles takes the view that, long before 1625, it was Herbert's intention to be ordained.

It is possible that the prospect of secular preferment tempted Herbert to abandon a long-term plan to enter the church. In any case there is ample evidence in his poems of a struggle with worldly ambition and of uncertainty about what to do with his life.

> *Now I am here, what thou wilt do with me*
> *None of my books will show:*
> *I reade, and sigh, and wish I were a tree;*
> *For sure I then should grow*
> *To fruit or shade . . .*

('Affliction')

Herbert had been writing poems since he was a teenager. At the beginning of 1610, aged seventeen, he sent his mother two sonnets with a letter saying, 'My meaning is in these Sonnets to declare my resolution to be, that my poor Abilities in Poetry, shall be all, and ever consecrated to God's glory.' 'Affliction' and other poems in which he expresses doubts and worries about his future were probably written between 1624, when he left Cambridge, and 1630 when he settled at Bemerton in Wiltshire and was, at last, ordained as a priest.

The little church of St Andrew at Bemerton still stands today, on a traffic island in a suburb of Salisbury. Across the road is the rectory where Herbert lived with his wife, Jane, whom he had married in 1629. The River Nadder runs at the bottom of the garden.

Twice a week, Herbert walked along the riverside to Salisbury Cathedral to hear evensong, an experience he described as his 'Heaven upon Earth'. After a lifetime of ill health, he died in Bemerton rectory on 1 March 1633, aged thirty-nine, and was buried in St Andrew's Church two days later.

None of his poems in English had appeared in print during his lifetime. When he was dying he arranged for his handwritten book of them to be taken to his friend Nicholas Ferrar, the founder of the religious community at Little Gidding. This was his message to Ferrar: 'If he think it may turn to the advantage of any dejected poor soul, let it be made public; if not, let him burn it.' By the end of 1633, the book was in print.

Entitled *The Temple*, it was an immediate success – four editions were published in three years. In the ensuing decades, Herbert's appeal extended across the religious divide that was soon to tear the nation apart. His work was admired by Anglicans (including King Charles) and by Puritans on both sides of the Atlantic. Numerous poets, of whom the most distinguished was Henry Vaughan, attempted to imitate him.

He was less highly regarded in the eighteenth century, and no new editions appeared between 1709 and 1799. In the nineteenth century, Herbert was championed by Coleridge and Ruskin and, in America, by Emerson. Opinion as to the value of his work continued to be divided until the 1930s, when Eliot made a very influential contribution to the debate. Since then his reputation has been secure.

As I go about my daily life, phrases from 'The Church Porch', the first section of Herbert's poem 'The Temple', often come to mind. On Sundays it is 'Judge Not the Preacher', an instruction I am unable to comply with. At the beginning of a new poetry notebook I write 'Dare to be true' from one of Herbert's stanzas on honesty. But the lines most worth remembering are the two that form the final couplet of 'The Church Porch':

If thou do ill; the joy fades, not the pains:
If well; the pain doth fade, the joy remains.

Herbert's reputation rests chiefly on the poems in the middle section of *The Temple*, entitled 'The Church'. Among these are his well-known pattern poems, 'The Altar' (in which the lines are arranged into the shape of an altar) and 'Easter-Wings'. With this poem a choice has to be made between printing it so that it looks like two butterflies – in which case the reader has to turn the book sideways to read it – or printing it with the words the right way up. The stanzas then look like hourglasses, another appropriate image for a poem about decay and renewal. Herbert didn't invent the pattern poem but when he had a go at it the results were better than most.

Any reader of Herbert will be struck by the variety of forms he uses, and by his skill in finding appropriate forms for his subject matter. In a poem called 'A Wreath', he uses repetition so that the lines imitate their subject, overlapping and coming full circle to where he began. 'Trinitie Sunday' consists of three tercets (three-line stanzas) and ends with a line containing three verbs: 'That I may runne, rise, rest with thee.'

Dr Julia Carolyn Guernsey, in her book *The Pulse of Praise*, argues that the relationship between Herbert and his god is analogous to the relationship between the child and the 'good-enough' mother described in the work of the psychoanalyst Donald Winnicott. I have found this a helpful way of looking at the poems. The god who causes Herbert, in several of his poems, to grieve and complain when he seems to be absent, does, in other poems, resemble a good and loving parent.

This is certainly true in 'Love' (also known as 'Love (III)' because Herbert wrote two other poems with that title):

> Love bade me welcome: yet my soul drew back,
>   Guiltie of dust and sinne.
> But quick-ey'd Love, observing me grow slack
>   From my first entrance in,
> Drew nearer to me, sweetly questioning,
>   If I lack'd anything.

As the speaker continues to insist on his unworthiness, 'Love', or Christ, patiently encourages him to 'sit down' and 'taste my meat', eventually overcoming his reluctance: 'So I did sit and eat.'

The greatest difficulty for a poet, says Eliot, is to distinguish between 'what one really feels and what one would like to feel'. I have been quoting those wise words for years. It was only very recently that I discovered they come from an article on George Herbert. Eliot thought him 'as secure, as habitually sure as any poet who has written in English' at avoiding 'moments of falsity'.

Herbert himself says something similar to Eliot's dictum in one of my favourite poems, 'A True Hymne'. In the first stanza he complains that he can't think of anything to write except these words, 'My joy, my life, my crown.' This is the second stanza:

Yet slight not these few words:
If truly said, they may take part
Among the best in art.
The fitnesse which a hymne or psalme affords,
Is, when the soul unto the lines accords.

And these lines are from the last stanza:

Whereas if the heart be moved
Although the verse be somewhat scant,
God doth supply the want.

Introduction to 'George Herbert: Verse and Prose (a selection)',
SPCK 2002, abridged for publication in the Guardian

By Chance

About fifteen years ago while I was teaching a summer course at the Skyros Centre in Greece I picked up a discarded paperback copy of *An Evil Cradling* by Brian Keenan. It's his account of his four-and-a-half years as a hostage in Beirut and his friendship with fellow hostage John McCarthy. I might not have thought of buying it because I thought I knew enough about this episode from newspapers, radio and television. And I had no reason to think that Keenan was an especially good writer – I must have missed the reviews. By the time I'd read twenty or thirty pages I was glad to have come across it by chance. It's a powerful and moving book, very well written. In 1991 it won the *Irish Times* Literature Prize for non-fiction. By the time I finished it I felt warm admiration for the author.

A few months later, having parked my car in a London street, I came back to find a motorcycle parked so close to it that there was no way I was going to get out of the space. As I stood there wondering what to do, a man came out of a nearby theatre and saw the problem. He picked up the motorbike and moved it several yards down the street. I thanked him. He nodded, smiled and went on his way. I recognised the man from his photographs. It was Brian Keenan.

Daily Telegraph 2014

Settee Life

This section consists largely of television columns I wrote for the Spectator between 1986 and 1990. Jenny Naipaul, who was the magazine's arts editor at the time, wrote the titles and I saw no need to change them.

The opening piece explains how I got the job and updates my tastes in television to 2005, when I wrote it. In 2014, I still watch University Challenge *every week when it's on. Two or three times I have been the answer to a question, which made my day. The only time I envied Andrew Motion during his laureateship was when he presented the trophy at the end of a series. A couple of years later I was invited to do the same thing – and without having to be poet laureate.*

Despite my fear of being on television, I couldn't refuse.

These days, as in the past, some of my favourite programmes are American. My mother-in-law alerted me to The Good Wife, *a series about lawyers, which hides away on More 4 and is an absolute must. I adore* Mad Men *but have to catch up with box sets since it emigrated to Sky Atlantic. The British programmes I watch are mainly crime stories –* Lewis, Midsomer Murders *(ridiculous but watchable),* Vera, *and a few others. A couple of Christmases ago an unfortunate thing happened to Lachlan and me. Forced by relatives to watch* EastEnders *and* Coronation Street, *we became addicted. We're still watching them. I don't know how long this is going to last. I sit there grumbling: 'completely implausible', 'entirely out of character', 'too much plot'. However, I was glad not to have missed the storyline in* Coronation Street *about Hayley's death. That was brilliantly done – as good as anything I've seen in any kind of television drama.*

Couch Potato

Once upon a time I was a bit of a couch potato, and, by chance, I found a cure. In 1986, Charles Moore, then editor of the *Spectator*, offered me the job of television critic. The offer came just after I had given up my day job to go freelance, so I couldn't afford to refuse. My attitude to television changed overnight. Watching the box was no longer a pleasurable self-indulgence, but something I was supposed to do, unwelcome drudgery that kept me from my preferred pastimes of reading books and listening to music.

In fact, I didn't have to watch very much. The television columnist of the *Spectator*, paid a modest weekly fee, is not expected to treat the position as a full-time job. Charles said I could review the test card, as long as I wrote something interesting about it. That was fine. But no one had explained to the publicity departments of the television companies that I was not a full-time employee on a fat salary. They rang me every day, urging me to go to previews, telling me I really ought to watch this or that programme, offering to send me tapes. Bumf arrived in the post about programme after programme that was far too important to miss. Too often I caved in and watched whatever they were pushing.

Sometimes their efforts were counter-productive. The fanfare of publicity for *The Singing Detective* was such that I decided to give it a miss. I knew all the other television critics would review it and thought my readers might be glad of something different. It soon became clear that I was the only member of the chattering classes not watching Dennis Potter's drama, which was something of a disadvantage on social occasions.

The job lasted four years, until Charles moved on. His successor sent for me and told me I wasn't nasty enough. A few weeks later, when I had failed to improve in this respect, he sacked me. At first I was cross and offended but that quickly gave way to a realisation that I had been liberated. Bliss! I would never have to watch television again.

For a few years I watched very little. Gradually I began to enjoy it again, in small doses. Occasionally, to my surprise, I have found myself wishing I still had the column because there is an opinion I would like to express. For example, I am glad of an opportunity to say that the best thing on television in recent years, by a mile, was *Six Feet Under*, the American drama series about a family of undertakers. It was funny, wise, and sexy, and it avoided cliché at every turn. I say 'was' because, if it is being broadcast at all now, it is on some non-terrestrial channel that we can't get.

The same is true of my second favourite, *The West Wing*. This is special in our household because it is one of the few programmes that my partner and I watch together – he is obsessed with American politics. Every episode includes at least one schmaltzy scene, which causes my companion to wipe a tear from his eye. He does it surreptitiously because, if I see the handkerchief come out, I laugh at him.

In my reviewing days, when my favourite programme was *L.A. Law*, my preference for American dramas annoyed British television people. It hasn't changed. Sometimes, after an especially fast and witty exchange of dialogue in *The West Wing*, I say, 'Wow. You'd never get anything like that in a British programme.' You have to be intelligent to follow *The West Wing*. You have to concentrate. Now and again we need to wind the tape back because, what with the accents and the pace, we haven't caught what they said. But that's OK. I'm grateful not to be patronised.

The third American drama series I have to mention is *Desperate Housewives*. I'm not sure that it needs the melodramatic plot with all the murders but I love it anyway – the women and their clothes and their relationships. It is in a different league from the horrible and tacky *Footballers' Wives*, as I have sometimes had to explain to people who confuse the two.

None of the favourites mentioned above is currently available, and I like to have something to watch late in the evening, as a way of winding down. Some days it's just the BBC news at 10 p.m. On Mondays I record *University Challenge* and then record or watch *Without a Trace*, the American series about the FBI Missing Persons Bureau. It isn't wonderful but it will do. Tuesdays, Wednesdays and Thursdays offer very little at present. I have not been watching *Bleak House* because they've changed it and left out some of the characters. On Fridays there's *Taggart*, which is still just about watchable after all these years, though not unmissable. Being British, it takes ninety minutes to tell a story that the Americans would whizz through in an hour.

In the last three months Saturday has been my big television night because I am addicted, as I was last year, to *The X Factor*. I have to watch it early in the evening, when it is broadcast, so I can vote for my favourites. This can involve making as many as six expensive phone calls. An hour later I switch on again to learn the result. A couple of weeks ago I had to stop voting because I really liked everyone who was left, and there was no point in voting for all of them. I was sad to see Chico go, and almost in tears when Brenda, the last remaining woman, sang her farewell number. At the time of writing, the final is still ahead. It will be painful because I want everybody to win.

Though I sometimes enjoy the songs, the point of *The X Factor* is not so much the music as the people. It is interesting to see who the viewing public will vote for. That was my excuse for watching three series of *Big Brother*. If the nice people did well, it reinforced my faith in human nature. My favourite *Big Brother* was the one that starred Cameron the Christian and was condemned by the press as boring. I liked Cameron and I was bowled over by his courage and originality, going on a reality show and reading the Bible to his fellow contestants. After that the programme-makers decided they had to find inmates who were louder, zanier and more quarrelsome. Great. It has become so appalling that I am freed from any urge to watch it.

2005 for a national newspaper. Can't remember or find out which one.

Personal Property

The first time I watched *Dallas*, many moons ago, it took me about ten minutes to decide that it was very low-grade garbage indeed. I switched off, confident that I would never again feel tempted to waste any time on it. One evening a few weeks later I went to see some friends, who, unusually for them, refused to turn off the television. And so it came about that I was forcibly exposed to a full fifty-minute episode of *Dallas*. I have been hopelessly hooked ever since.

To begin with I felt ashamed but I cheered up when I realised what good company I was in. My colleagues at work, the television critics of the posh newspapers, a well-known feminist novelist, and my Freudian psycho-analyst, to mention but a few. I asked the shrink why he liked the programme. 'The women are very pretty,' he replied, 'and J.R. is an interesting character.' I could see that if you spent all day listening to neurotics with overactive superegos, J.R. Ewing would come as something of a relief.

In the current series J.R.'s wife, Sue Ellen, has been recovering from one of her alcoholic phases and there has been a great deal of emphasis on her need to be her own person. This expression has always puzzled me and I worry about not being able to grasp its exact meaning. Am I my own person? Anyone who watches American television programmes will appreciate that this is a very important question, especially for women. Is there any hope for a person who doesn't know what being one's own person means? Or is it because I have never been anybody else's person that I fail to understand the concept? I am not sure.

In Sue Ellen's case the quest for own-personhood has meant turning down an offer of marriage from her long-lost love, Dusty Farlow, and taking a job at a glossy new medical research centre. There she has met an even nicer, better-looking, brighter and probably richer man called Dr Jerry Kenderson and now he wants to marry her as well. It amounts to a persuasive argument for BOOP.

Jenna, too, has been having a difficult time lately. In bedrooms all over Dallas, couples have been telling each other that they are worried about Jenna. They could tell how serious her problem was because she refused to talk about it for four or five episodes. One of the appealing things about this fantasy world, along with the expensive clothes, swimming-pools and expensive restaurants, is the way that anyone who looks a bit gloomy for five minutes is tenderly encouraged to say what is bothering them. And if someone announces a need to talk, it is given the same kind of priority that needing an ambulance gets in real life.

By last week Jenna was much better, as she told Bobby when she went to his grave for a chat. Being dead, around Southfork, is not considered a good enough reason for ceasing to listen to other people's problems. There are rumours that Bobby will not be dead much longer and it will be intriguing, if Patrick Duffy does rejoin the cast, to see how the scriptwriters get round the fact that he has been six feet under for several months. I think it is now too late for anyone to notice a faint knocking sound when they change the flowers. My guess is that Bobby came to in the mortuary of Dallas General Hospital and decided to disappear for a while. Or perhaps he will turn out to have been separated at birth from an identical twin brother ('Why didn't you tell us, Momma?') Either story would be hard to swallow but at least we shan't be asked to accept a new Bobby Ewing with a different face.

The only time I came close to going off the programme was when Barbara Bel Geddes was ill and they drafted in someone else to play Miss Ellie. What they should have done was to send the Ewing matriarch on a long trip until Miss Geddes was better. Then we could have had a heartwarming scene when she came home, with tears in her eyes, to tell them all that she cared about them, that she needed to talk to them, and that she was her own person now.

Spectator 1986

Marathon Moments

In a recent edition of *Write On* (Channel 4) the poet Ian McMillan made an admirable attempt to demystify poetry. 'People come to me and say, "I can't write a *poem*." I say, "OK. Don't write a poem. Write a settee."' You don't, he explained, have to call it a poem. If the idea is threatening, just call it something else instead.

I like this liberated approach and I wish I could make use of it. I would feel a lot more relaxed about what I am writing now if I could think of it as a settee or a toast-rack or a three-drawer bureau, finished in walnut veneer with mahogany-effect knobs. But there is no getting away from the fact that at the end of the day it has got to be a television column. 'Settee Life' would be rather a good name for it.

During my recent break from settee life I spent a weekend in the country and played darts in the pub all Saturday evening. I enjoyed this tremendously, even though my partner and I lost every single game. Full of new-found enthusiasm, I watched *Championship Darts* on BBC 2 last week and discovered that what we lost were not games but legs. At the end of the evening we were legless. On television male darts players sometimes have vintage legs to go with their vintage paunches. Lady players are patronised by the commentators, just like in the pub.

Although I have never been at all keen on sport, I have found over the years that it is possible to get involved in almost any event if you watch it for long enough on television. Watching golf with my mother, for example, I was surprised to discover that after about half an hour it became utterly gripping. From time to time I have been briefly addicted to cricket, ice dancing, snooker, showjumping and even, during the 1966 World Cup (I can scarcely believe this now), to football.

Fifty Not Out (BBC 1), a compilation of the highlights of half a century of televised sport, sounded as if it might be fun. I taped all two hours of it but only managed to watch the first forty minutes or so, giving up in the middle of a stretch about boxing. The problem, perhaps inevitable with a programme of this kind, was that there wasn't enough time to get interested in anything. Two or three minutes each of the Wembley Olympics, the Rome Olympics, the Tokyo Olympics. One minute of Torvill and Dean. There were some good moments, however. I was glad to be reminded, by Peter Dimmock, of the expression 'I made a complete Horlicks of it.' And I shall never tire of the film of the best-ever Boat Race, in which one of the commentators ventures the opinion that 'Cambridge are having a much easier passage than Oxford', while the Oxford boat disappears beneath the surface of the Thames. His colleague had a better grasp of the situation: 'And there you have a very unusual view indeed of a crew in the Boat Race sinking. It hasn't happened since 1925.'

Making fun of sports commentators has itself become something of a national sport, especially when the commentator is David Coleman. One hardly likes to join the pack but he makes it difficult to resist. Early in *Fifty Not Out* Coleman showed viewers the latest lightweight television camera. 'It really does,' he claimed, 'give new meaning to the expression in the trade, "hand-held".' What, I wondered, was the old meaning of that esoteric bit of jargon?

Spectator 1986

Boiled to an Epic

Back in the Sixties, when one of my flatmates applied for a job with an advertising agency, she was asked to make a list of all the uses she could think of for a teacup. This was called a creativity test and I think she did quite well. One of her ideas was that if you needed a little extra height to reach something, you could put a teacup upside down on the floor and stand on it. Impressed though I was by her creativity, I have never had occasion to try this and I bet she hasn't either.

The teacup test came to mind last week as I looked forward to Sunday's edition of *Thinking Aloud* (BBC 2), in which the question to be discussed was 'What Use is Poetry?' I am not sure why this question makes me smile – perhaps because it seems to imply that poetry may not be any use at all. What are we to do about poetry, if we can't think of any uses for it? Fortunately it is not difficult to see that poetry is useful in all sorts of ways. You can decorate trays and biscuit tins with it, print it on calendars, display it on underground trains and carve it on paving stones on the South Bank. You can improve the tone of your bookshelves by buying volumes of it. You can earn money by reviewing it, judging it, teaching it and reciting it. You can use it to fill awkward spaces in newspapers and magazines and to entertain listeners during concert intervals on Radio 3. This much is obvious. Not everyone realises, however, that you can use poetry to time the boiling of an egg. A sonnet plus a limerick, spoken at average speed, take about a minute. An alternative method is to forget about the minute as a unit of measurement and ask the family at what point in, say, *The Rime of the Ancient Mariner* or *The Jumblies*, they would like their eggs removed from the saucepan.

None of these ideas came up in *Thinking Aloud*, described in its publicity leaflet as 'the most serious discussion programme on television'. The chairperson, Michael Ignatieff, talks like this: 'Let's leave the definitional question here with a kind of notional idea that the bottom line, in crude language, is music and meaning and an exploration of music and meaning as what is essential for what poetry is all about.' But he has a nice smile and a charming manner. In the only other *Thinking Aloud* I have seen, he discussed 'Writers and Power' with three French intellectuals – Bernard-Henri Lévy, Alain Finkielkraut, and Dan Sperber. They were so very French and intellectual that they looked as if they might get up and bite each other at any moment. Sunday night's discussion – with poets Fred D'Aguiar and Peter Porter and academic Gillian Beer – was more amiable and relaxed. The talk ranged over a number of topics – why people write poetry, what poetry is, language and dialect, oral and printed cultures, poetry and politics, the audience. The advertised question didn't get much of a look-in but I didn't think this mattered at all. What mattered was that all three guests had some interesting things to say and got the opportunity to say them. They also made a few humorous remarks which, paradoxically, helped me not to regard the whole thing as a joke.

A programme that takes itself as seriously as *Thinking Aloud* does is inevitably in danger of being unintentionally comic. All the same, I approve of it. As Peter Porter said of poetry, 'If you take it away, something worse will take its place.'

Spectator 1986

Dance and Drama

The programmes have got better this week, a mixed blessing from my point of view, because now there is even more that I feel I ought to watch. Television used to be an indulgence, something to enjoy when I was tired or not very well or doing the ironing. All that has changed, now that I have to concentrate and take notes. Of course, it is extremely nice, as work goes, and I mustn't grumble. I'll just have to find a new way of relaxing.

Dance, perhaps. The final programme in the series *The Healing Arts* (BBC 2) showed a dance therapist called Wolfgang Stange working with cardiac patients at Charing Cross Hospital. Although both the patients and their doctors spoke convincingly about the benefits of this kind of therapy, I thought some of it looked as if it might be difficult to take seriously. At one point, for example, a large red cloth was solemnly draped over a tableau of patients and oriental masks were balanced on their protruding hands and knees. But nobody got the giggles and when they all lay down on the floor at the end of the session, looking immensely happy and peaceful, I found myself wondering if Wolfgang runs any classes for those of us who haven't had a heart attack yet.

One of the children in Deborah Moggach's *To Have and to Hold* (ITV) wanted to join a different kind of dancing class.

'Mum, why can't I do ballet?' she asked.

'Because you do dance.'

'I want to do ballet in a ballet dress.'

'Ballet's regressive,' muttered her parent, who at least had the grace to sound embarrassed.

Sharply observed, I thought. Small girls with an instinct for what will upset their trendy parents are always good value and I have sometimes got into trouble for laughing when one of them demands a yellow net party dress or a plastic pencil case featuring a picture of a girly girl with a ponytail. Moggach's characterisation of the unpleasant public-school husband was also well done and the interaction between him and the lower-middle-class in-laws would have made any sensitive person cringe. Towards the end of the first episode, however, there were signs that this high standard is not going to be maintained. When the real theme of the series – surrogate motherhood – lumbered into view, we got some yucky speeches and a sentimental song to go with the credits.

A person from Dumbarton has written to tell me that he only reads this column to drive himself to a fury and that I am just as bad as Richard Ingrams and Peter Levi. 'Honestly dear,' he continues, 'to read a woman producing the same kind of drivel as those two – it's too much.' I take this as a compliment, undeserved but encouraging,

and I shall do my best to go on annoying the gentleman.
Honestly dear.

Spectator 1986

On the Ball

I rarely watch football or glance at the sports pages but I had acquired some background information before switching on *Match of the Day Live* (BBC 1) on Sunday. It was provided by one helpful friend and it can be summarised as follows. Tottenham Hotspur are the best team. Their motto 'Audere est facere' is very appropriate, unlike the names of their players, who are mostly called Hoddle, Waddle and Toddle. ('There isn't a Toddle,' he says irritably, every time I make this joke.) Arsenal, on the other hand, are terrible. In the last few months this boring bunch of no-hopers has somehow reached first place in the league table, thereby depriving Spurs of their rightful position at the top of everything.

Just in case any Arsenal supporters read the *Spectator* (although if the things I have been told about them are true, this does not seem at all likely) I had better add that I realise my source is biased. However, I did allow myself to be persuaded that the live coverage of the 100th North London derby was going to be the most unmissable programme of the week. By the end of last week I was actually looking forward to it and quite downcast when it looked as if it would be called off because of the strike.

My first disappointment was that there wasn't enough build-up and razzmatazz. I had expected, on such an important occasion, a long stretch of scene-setting and studio discussion to help me get in the mood. Apparently you get more of that sort of thing on ITV. All we got on BBC 1 was five minutes of Jimmy Hill (who looks astonishingly like Bruce Forsyth these days) and Trevor Brooking (who looks as if he should be smoking a pipe and starring in a 1950s war film). Trevor thought Spurs would win and Jimmy plumped for Arsenal. By the time we went over to White Hart Lane the teams were coming out onto the pitch. After the match I heard all about the parade of ex-players and how the crowd sang 'Nice One Cyril' for Cyril Knowles and gave Danny Blanchflower a standing ovation. I would have loved all that but they didn't broadcast it.

The second disappointment was the much-derided commentator John Motson. He seemed perfectly OK and didn't make me laugh at all. My friend thinks John Motson is a secret Arsenal supporter but I couldn't see much reason for going along with this. In some quarters, no doubt, he is thought of as a secret supporter of Everton, Liverpool, Manchester City, and Manchester United and possibly even of Spurs. He has a difficult job.

But the match itself was pretty gripping, despite my limited understanding of what was going on. John Motson doesn't have time to explain the rules for the benefit of people like me, so I am still confused about offside and corners and free kicks and whether a professional foul is better or worse than an unprofessional one. It didn't matter. I still got caught up in the atmosphere and, if not actually roaring with the crowd, was at least bouncing up and down on the settee when Mitchell Thomas finally put one away for Spurs. By this time, I am afraid to say, Arsenal had two goals to their credit. 'Tottenham have impressed me today,' commented Bobby Charlton, 'because they haven't thrown in the towel even though they've been under the gun.' Absolutely. In the second half there were no more goals but Spurs kept looking as if they might score one any minute and the crowd roared and chanted even louder. It wasn't possible to catch many of the words and I realised, when I was told what the Spurs fans had been calling Charlie Nicholas, that it was probably just as well.

At six o'clock one dejected Spurs supporter arrived at my front door and we watched edited highlights on the video, leaving out the bits where Arsenal scored. I said it was a pity there hadn't been any interviews after the match, with people saying they felt sick as a parrot or over the moon. Nowadays, I was informed, they don't say those things any more. They say, 'Well, on the day, Barry, it just didn't seem to go right.' Next time I decide to watch a football match I shall pick one on the other channel. I don't just want to see the action – I want all the trimmings as well.

Spectator 1987

Fine Figures

'Hating numbers, they rattle down to zero.' This line by Michael Hofmann has been rattling round my head all week. It comes at the end of a poem entitled 'Entropy (The Late Show)' which can be found in his first book, *Nights in the Iron Hotel*. The *Concise Oxford Dictionary* defines entropy thus: 'Measure of the unavailability of a system's thermal energy for conversion into mechanical work.' It is a good title for a poem about watching darts on television.

Late one night, my thermal energy unavailable for anything more strenuous, I picked up my pocket calculator and worked out the minimum number of throws needed to win a game. I made it nine. Several players in *World Darts* (BBC 2) managed what the commentator calls 'an eleven-darter' but I don't think anyone did better than that. I also wanted to know which of the numbers over 160 could be demolished with three darts, ending on a bullseye. The answer seems to be 161, 164, 167 and 170. That is why they kept referring to 166 as 'a bogey number'. Two players in the championship, Jocky Wilson and John Lowe, each won a game by scoring 161 (treble 19, treble 18, bull) and they share a £1,000 prize for doing so. I have yet to see a 170 check-out. That, along with a nine-darter, is something to look forward to. It is a long time since I last felt this keen on arithmetic and it occurs to me that there is a lot to be said for having a dartboard in every primary school classroom. On the other hand there is a lot to be said against it.

To enjoy watching any sport, you need to care who wins. This, I suppose, is why athletics commentators talk in an excited way about England winning the bronze. They hope that patriotism will give us a reason for being interested. In darts the seeded players are almost all English. The Scots and the Welsh may have been rooting for Jocky Wilson and Alan Evans but the rest of us needed to choose our favourites on some other basis than nationality. I decided to support the fatter of the two players in each match. The shape and size of the contestants is one of the appealing things about this game. It is very gratifying to see an overweight individual fighting his way towards a sporting title, especially if he has a cigarette in his hand. My preference for the larger girth only wavered when it got to the final. John Lowe, who has lost forty-eight pounds on a diet of prawn sandwiches, is now less paunchy than Eric Bristow. But Lowe has a nice face and Bristow, the Björn Borg of darts, had already won the championship five times. It was a great match. Some of the most enthralling moments in darts are those when a player does the kind of thing you or I might do, such as missing a double five with three consecutive throws. If his opponent, stepping forward to claim an obvious victory, also misses the double three times, the tension becomes unbearable. You tug at your hair, you slap your thigh, you groan out loud. You cannot believe that you can get into this state about a game of darts. Thank goodness it is over. John Lowe, by the way, is the new world champion.

The timing of the darts championship has been fortuitous. It must have provided a focus of interest for many old people stranded by the weather, as well as for those of us who could perfectly well have gone out but chose not to. And presumably it was just the luck of the duty rota that brought Ian McCaskill to our screens every evening last week. It takes a very special kind of *je ne sais quoi* to make me smile and smile while I am being told that the weather will continue to be lousy. Readers of this column have been spared a longer rhapsody about my favourite weather forecaster only because Alan Rusbridger got in first with several paragraphs in last Sunday's *Observer*. I will merely add that when McCaskill comes on the screen and says hello, I sometimes say hello back. No one else on television has this effect on me. I hope it isn't a symptom of premature senility.

Spectator 1987

Ageing Beautifully

'Whatever happens,' said a friend of mine fifteen years ago, 'at least we'll never be any older than Mick Jagger.' It was a comforting thought at the time but it aroused mixed feelings on Saturday as I watched the *Whistle Test Special* on the Rolling Stones (BBC 2). We are, it is true, still younger than Mick but I am not at all sure that anyone would guess it to look at us. On the other hand it is encouraging to see someone in his forties dancing around like that and getting away with it. Mick is doing pretty well and perhaps we are not irrevocably past it either.

How does he manage it? I don't suppose he relies on *Slimming* magazine's *Your Greatest Guide to Calories*, a publication I have given to one or two men friends who are worried about their weight. They wouldn't be seen dead buying such a thing from a newsagent but they find it very educational, usually expressing surprise when they discover how many calories there are in a pint of beer.

The question of eating and drinking habits didn't come up in the programme, but there was a certain amount of talk about hobbies. This was because the presenter, David Hepworth, had decided he wanted to make a point about some of the Stones living just for the group, while others had outside interests. He was determined to keep on bringing this up, even though the reaction of his subjects suggested that it was the kind of question they had got bored with long ago.

'I don't spend my time doing fretwork or anything,' said Keith Richards, wearily massaging his neck as he spoke.

Later on Hepworth asked Charlie Watts what he did in between making records.

'Nothing,' replied Charlie.

'I understand,' the interviewer persisted, 'that you collect things.'

'Yeah. That's easy, innit?'

Charlie, a reluctant interviewee if ever I saw one, gave Hepworth a hard time right up to the moment when he decided to bring the interview to an end. Then the drummer relented for a minute or two and the ghost of a smile appeared on his face as he informed us that his twenty-five years with the Rolling Stones had consisted of five years' work and twenty years' hanging around.

Spectator 1986

Feminism and Fiddles

I think the first Country and Western song I ever learned must have been 'A Four-Legged Friend'. If I remember rightly, it was sung by Roy Rogers. The gist of it is that a four-legged friend will always be faithful and never let you down. It was taught to me by my sister, who enjoyed cowboy films, and we used to sing it very loudly. It was especially satisfying when you were fed up with all your two-legged friends and relations.

I recalled this childhood favourite as a result of watching *An A–Z of C & W* on Channel 4. As it happens, I know very little about this kind of music and I am confused about definitions. Are there three different categories – Country, Western and Country-and-Western? And how does one tell the difference? I suppose it is safe to assume that anything with a cowboy in it must be Western but that is as far as I can go towards clarifying the matter. After watching one and a half television programmes on the subject I am not much wiser but I am beginning to feel quite enthusiastic.

An A–Z is presented by a wonderfully eccentric English doctor called Sam Hutt, known to the C & W world as Hank Wangford. Hank has a ponytail and a lot of stubble on his face and he dresses in cowboy gear. He speaks with an English accent when he is interviewing Americans and with an American accent when he appears on stage with his group. I don't know how he presents himself to his patients but I am sure he cheers them up.

The alphabetical format of his programmes – with sections on, for example, Fans, Feminism and Fiddles – seems bitty and confusing at times but at least there is no opportunity to get bored. Long interviews with Bobby Bare and Loretta Lynn, which might well try my patience if they were shown whole, have been cut into tolerable pieces and interspersed through the series. For personal reasons, I was interested to see Loretta Lynn dealing with the inevitable silly question about feminism. 'You seem,' ventured the interviewer, 'to sing from the point of view of sisterhood, rather than Feminism with a capital F.' I groaned in sympathy but Loretta seemed not to mind. 'That's what I tell them,' she replied. 'They would come to me as if I was a women's libber and I'd say, "Hold it. You don't see me out there burnin' my bra." You know? I'm wearing my bra. And I'm for women but I'm not against men. That's for sure.'

Last year an interviewer asked me if I would describe myself as a feminist but not the kind of feminist who was aggressive about men. No I wouldn't, I said. In my view, being aggressive about men was just fine – what I couldn't stand was the lentil-eating, goddess-worshipping kind of feminism. I thought this was rather a brave thing to say to the *Guardian* but, after I had been boasting about it for a week, the goddess got her own back. My little joke was garbled and the piece appeared under a headline saying, 'She is a non-lentil worshipping feminist'. I have been looking for a chance to set the record straight and I hope readers will forgive the digression. To return to Loretta Lynn, I can't help thinking that the author of a song called 'Your Squaw Is on the Warpath Tonight' must be the teeniest bit against men now and then.

Spectator 1987

Postman's Weather

'Remember your television cannot listen to you, nor reply.' This useful piece of advice from Dr Anthony Fry, consultant psychiatrist at Guy's Hospital, was published in the *Independent* last week. It is part of Dr Fry's prescription for survival in a threatening world. I thought I should mention it here for the benefit of any readers who are still trying to establish a rapport with their sets.

I don't think I often forget that the television can't hear me but that doesn't always prevent me from speaking to it. Until recently it was just a question of a friendly 'Hello' to Ian McCaskill, or the occasional 'Kick him', addressed to a female character in a play or drama series. However, it got worse during the election campaign, when remarks such as 'Come on, surprise me' or 'I would never have expected you to say that' were frequently directed at my impervious screen. At the time it made me feel better but so do a number of other things that are bad for my health.

Eating fried bread is one of them. I was prompted to do this by the first act of Harold Pinter's *The Birthday Party* (BBC 2), in which Mrs Bowles serves the delicacy to her husband and the lodger for breakfast. They didn't seem terribly thrilled with it but I couldn't concentrate until I had gone out to the kitchen and made myself a piece for the first time in months. I had fried bread for breakfast on Monday morning as well. If I regain all the weight I lost earlier this summer, I shall blame Pinter and the BBC. I don't think I had seen the play before. It was funnier than I expected and not only because parts of it sounded like a particularly brilliant Pinter parody. However, there were stretches where I glanced at my watch, experiencing that guilty feeling that comes from being able to see that something is good and hoping it won't go on too much longer.

Hardly anything in the week's television has given me as much pleasure as the mental picture, garnered from last week's *Spectator*, of Peter Levi watching *Postman Pat* (ITV). I watched a few episodes some months ago, vaguely thinking I might review it. The programme gave me a new expression, 'Postman Pat weather'. This means weather bad enough to cause serious inconvenience. Almost all Pat's problems are the result of the weather – snow one week, fog or wind the next – but, despite the appalling Green Dale climate, he goes on being happy. A non-smoking teetotaller who doesn't talk to television sets, Pat can teach us something about survival in a threatening world.

Spectator 1987

Seeing the Funny Side

Last week I remembered to watch *Loving Memory* (BBC 2), the second of Tony Harrison's programmes about the rituals that help us to deal with death. Reflecting on possible reasons why I forgot it the week before, I decided it was not so much because the subject might be depressing as because I am irritated by the idea of television people persuading poets to write to order. This attitude is the result of too many telephone calls from people with bright ideas for things they would like me to write, and I admit it is a bit irrational. Although poets need to be on their guard against churning out verse for money, there is no doubt that commissions sometimes stimulate good work.

Judging by the programme I saw – about funeral customs in Naples – this commission has worked out very well. When Harrison first appeared on the screen, speaking lugubrious quatrains in a lugubrious Yorkshire voice, I had some doubts. However, they evaporated quite quickly. He wove all the necessary information into his poem with impeccable craft and at the same time struck exactly the right note, never patronising and some-times moving. 'Though there's no shame about it when they grieve/ And Mimmo's death broke everybody's heart,/ The prayers they make encourage him to leave –/ They need their dear departed to depart.' Does it work when it's written down? I think so, but it would be interesting to see the whole script. It is worth mentioning, for the benefit of anyone who hasn't discovered it already, that Tony Harrison has written a remarkable sequence of sonnets about his relationship with his parents and their deaths. This is included in his *Selected Poems*, published by Penguin.

Harrison, although he writes with respect of Neapolitans praying for the souls of the departed, makes it clear that he has no belief in life after death. On Friday night's *Wogan* (BBC 1) the Bishop of Durham took advantage of an opportunity to set the record straight about his views. 'I do not,' he told Terry, 'deny the risen Christ.' In my notebook I wrote, 'There is something very bizarre about this.' Of course, there is no reason why a bishop shouldn't appear on a down-market chat show and proclaim the risen Lord to ten times as many people as watch any religious programme. And if it did seem odd to see him cheered like a pop star as he walked onto the set, what of that? I have always stuck up for the Bishop of Durham because he manages to annoy both my evangelical relations and my High Church friends. All the same, I couldn't help feeling that the whole interview could have been a sketch from *Monty Python's Flying Circus*.

of the wonderful things about *Monty Python* it put you in a frame of mind that made every-on television seem equally funny. Once, confused by regional variations in the schedules, I sat and wept with laughter at the beginning of a programme called *A Cornishman's View of the North East*. After five minutes or so it dawned on me that this wasn't a *Python* sketch at all but a perfectly serious travelogue. I haven't, up to now, been watching the *Monty Python* repeats on BBC 1, perhaps because I was afraid they wouldn't seem funny any more. On Saturday night I found out that at least half of it is just as entertaining as ever. There was the sketch about the mosquito hunt ('You hate him, then you respect him. And then you kill him') and the one with Eric Idle and Michael Palin as two camp judges ('I used my butch voice'). And then there was Beethoven trying to compose his Fifth Symphony and being interrupted by Mrs Beethoven ('Ludwig, have you seen the sugar bowl?') I could almost be tempted to go out and buy the video.

I planned to watch Mrs Thatcher on *Favourite Things* (BBC 2) but I became absorbed in my favourite thing, viz. writing something that no one commissioned, and I missed the first ten minutes. Mrs Thatcher showed viewers some porcelain and Queen Victoria's sketchbook. She read some lines by Rupert Brooke and spoke about poached eggs on Bovril toast. But mostly she talked about being prime minister. That is really her favourite thing.

Spectator 1987

Academic Soap Opera

This, if I have understood the professor correctly, is a monologic discourse. It uses a single voice to express a single point of view. A dialogic discourse, on the other hand, introduces other voices and other points of view. Anyone wishing to weave these learned terms into everyday conversation should note that the 'g' is pronounced as in logic, rather than as in monologue. It doesn't seem logical to me but that's how it is.

A television programme that is written and narrated by one person is also a monologic discourse. *Big Words . . . Small Worlds* (Channel 4) began as one of these, with David Lodge presenting an account of a conference on linguistics and literary theory at the University of Strathclyde. About a third of the way through, however, the executive producer, Colin MacCabe, interrupted one of Lodge's pieces to camera and suggested that they try and make the programme more dialogic. From then on we got the heads in boxes. Some of them belonged to people who hadn't said much at the ence, others to people who hadn't been there at boxes were superimposed on Lodge's film after ished it. At the end of the programme, after the credits, we heard the following exchange between producer and presenter:

'Don't you think the interruptions really did make a kind of dialogic text of the programme?'

'Well, originally I didn't like the idea and I still don't like the idea.' Genuinely dialogic, you see.

It was ingenious and it reflected nicely what had happened at the conference. As David Lodge explained at the beginning, every conference has a plot. According to one contributor, the plot is much the same each time. At some point in the proceedings the audience gets fed up with listening to the authority figures on the platform and grows mutinous. A young man complained that nothing was being said about Thatcher and Reagan and the nuclear threat. Another regretted that the conference did not reflect the culture of Glasgow. Some people resented the presence of the television cameras. The main problem, however, seemed to be that the speakers had more opportunity to speak than everybody else and that this was unfair. 'It was like *Dallas*,' somebody said, 'and we were the cattle.'

Jacques Derrida, the star of the occasion, has a fine head of white hair and does look rather like the kind of man who might appeal to Miss Ellie. Apart from that, it wasn't very much like *Dallas*, although it might have been, if we had been able to see what was going on behind the scenes. In *Small World*, David Lodge's novel about academic conferences, the formal business of speeches and debate plays quite a small part. Restricted to this aspect in the television programme, he demonstrated that he is one of those people who can make pretty well anything interesting.

The *Brass Tacks* programme *Smoke Gets in Your Eyes* (BBC 2) could probably be described as a monologic discourse. Almost everyone selected to appear in it was of the opinion that smoking is terrible and disgusting and shouldn't be allowed, except possibly in the back garden. Some day they'll come out with a report saying that smoking in the back garden is bad for the flowers and vegetables and then I'll feel even more sorry for smokers than I do now. Meanwhile the focus is on smoking at work and the newly discovered danger from 'sidestream' smoke – the smoke that goes straight into the office atmosphere without first being filtered through the smoker's lungs.

One would have more sympathy with people who are worried about this if they displayed more understanding of the nature of nicotine addiction, in particular of the fact that a smoker can't be expected to work effectively in a place where smoking isn't allowed. Consideration and understanding are needed on both sides and to call people disgusting is no help at all. What enabled me to give up the habit was the realisation that I could go on loathing the campaigners without continuing to damage my health.

Spectator 1987

The Naked Truth

This week's piece has to be in several days before Christmas, so one thing it can't be about is the programmes broadcast during the festive season. Various ways of dealing with the challenge occurred to me – ringing up and trying to get out of it didn't work, the idea of a think-piece on 'Television in the Eighties' didn't appeal. Eventually I decided to write about television from a different angle and tell the story of some experiences inside the box.

My first brush with television people happened when I was a twenty-two-year-old teacher. A friend of mine had just got a job on a BBC current affairs programme and she needed guinea pigs for an item on slimming. All I had to do was try out a certain kind of slimming biscuit for six weeks and I would get paid for it. It sounded like easy money. The experiment was a complete nonsense. I stuck rigidly to my diet, for reasons that had nothing whatsoever to do with the virtues of the product – I just wanted to be thinner by the time I was on television.

At the end of six weeks a producer and crew came to my flat to film me stepping onto the scales. The producer, a nasty little man with blow-dried grey hair, was determined to persuade me to take my dress off for the camera. I was equally determined that I wasn't going to. If it happened now, I hope I would maintain a stony silence while showing the gentleman the door. But I was young and got upset attempting to justify myself. The completed film showed me standing on the scales in my best dress, followed by a number of older and larger ladies who had been inveigled into appearing in their underwear. The money turned out to be peanuts, even by the standards of a probationary teacher.

A few years later I was approached by the producer of *Music Time*, a useful BBC series for schools. He had heard that I encouraged children to compose their own music and wanted to feature some of it on the programme. This was very gratifying. The nine- and ten-year-olds in my class, needless to say, were beside themselves with joy at the idea of being on television, and it was established beyond all possible doubt that mine was the best class to be in, even though I was no good at art or football.

We composed two pieces for two different programmes. One was inspired by a child's poem about a tulip growing, the other by a boat-ride on the Regent's Park canal, suggested and paid for by the BBC. The second piece, at my insistence, involved the whole class. One group made up water music, others attempted to evoke the tunnel, the railway bridge, the aviary and the pirate ca͟   It was a good project but hard work.

͟he day of the recording the children, who had
͟there was no need to dress up, arrived at school
͟ of splendid outfits, ranging from exotic

beachwear to party dresses or velvet bow ties. We went to the Television Centre by coach and spent a long, long hot day under the studio lights. At one point the presenters popped in and said hello, before disappearing into the screened-off area where they were doing their bit. When the programme was broadcast, it looked as if they had organised the whole thing – you would never have known there was a teacher involved. I like to think the children learned something, and not just about the technicalities of the medium.

Nowadays it is quite difficult for anyone to persuade me to have anything to do with television. It is also quite difficult to find anyone who doesn't think it is insane ever to turn down an opportunity to be on it. The chances are that the producer of a book programme or chat show wouldn't try and get me to take my clothes off. But my distrust goes back a long way.

Spectator 1988

Keeping Out of Trouble

It's a quiet time of year, a good opportunity to stay home, do some work and avoid fattening food and drink. Dylan Thomas said that no one can write poetry for more than a few hours a day and that's why poets spend the rest of their time getting into trouble. In the dead of winter, television is quite an attractive alternative to trouble. I feel as if I've watched lots of it in the past seven days, though my idea of 'lots' adds up to about a third of the twenty-seven hours that, according to a new government report, the average citizen sees in a week.

Although I enjoyed the first episode of *The Contract* (ITV), I was in two minds about watching the rest. The British agent had gone off to East Germany to fetch the professor. Either he would get him out safely or he wouldn't. There were no mysteries to unravel, no moles to unmask. But I stayed with it and found the story of the attempt to cross the frontier quite gripping enough to sustain my interest for another two hours. In fact the last fifteen minutes were so exciting that I could hardly watch at all, managing only to peep at the screen intermittently. At times like this I hear my father's voice saying, 'It's all right. It's only actors pretending,' but that doesn't make much difference. Suspension of disbelief is a curious phenomenon.

The opener to the current series of *Tales of the Unexpected* (ITV) was based on 'The Colonel's Lady' by Somerset Maugham, updated to the 1980s and including a nice plug for the *Literary Review*. The lady in question is the author of a book of poems. On first seeing this volume, her husband, beautifully played by Joss Ackland, says, 'It's a bit thin. Not much work in it, I suppose.' When he opens it, he comments, 'Ah, poetry. Not much in my line, poetry.' He goes on to offer the opinion that it doesn't look like poetry because it is all chopped up and it doesn't rhyme. Then he recites 'The boy stood on the burning deck' to show her what his idea of a poem is. I knew she wasn't going to murder him because that wouldn't have been unexpected.

The husband of the central character in *Campaign* (BBC 2) has left home because he feels he counts for less than his wife's career in advertising. She certainly has to rush around a lot, and so do all her colleagues. Everyone was under so much pressure that the programme gave me a headache. It isn't yet clear why this woman is willing to sacrifice her family life for something as pointless as a career in advertising. Perhaps it is the money. If I were her, I'd sell the big house and get an easier job.

Spectator 1988

Celebrity Grill

In last Monday's *Guardian* a Tewkesbury firm advertised for a 'Middleweight Writer with Heavyweight Potential'. If they had meant it literally, I would have been a strong candidate for the job. Elizabeth Taylor, these days, is a lightweight writer with heavyweight potential and the subject of some of the most inspiring before-and-after pictures ever seen. For her appearance on *Aspel and Company* (ITV) to promote her book, she wore a tight-fitting purple dress with a wide black collar. It wasn't very pretty but it did show off to advantage both her figure and a whacking great diamond brooch that used to belong to the Duchess of Windsor.

At the beginning of the programme Michael Aspel announced that he had been a fan of Miss Taylor's ever since he wrote and asked for a signed photograph at the age of fourteen. This long-standing admiration didn't prevent him from getting straight down to the nitty-gritty with charmless directness. How much had she weighed? Of all the unkind remarks that had been made about her, which was the most hurtful? 'Don't answer,' I said, but she did.

It occurred to me, as it has before, that the celebrity

interview is evolving into a kind of public torture, inflicted on the successful out of a need for revenge. Most people I've discussed this with think that if someone agrees to be on television they are asking for it and anything goes. I can't concur with this view and I have an uneasy feeling that women interviewees get the worst of it. There they are, all dressed up and vulnerable, and here is a man asking questions that would make most people burst into tears. Michael Aspel asked some very probing questions about Miss Taylor's feelings for Richard Burton. They made me wince but she dealt with them extremely well, even managing some witty answers. Presumably she is used to it by now and goes through the routine on automatic pilot. But there was no warmth whatever in the way she looked at her self-proclaimed admirer.

Our chat shows, of course, have been greatly influenced by the American example. Happily the same is not true of our religious programmes, though not, it seems, for want of trying on the part of the evangelicals. Their attempts to obtain time on the airwaves were the subject of an excellent *Everyman* (BBC 1) entitled *Tell Us the Good News*. The good news, from my point of view, is that the evos are not getting anywhere. We were treated to a delicious encounter between John Whale, head of religious television at the BBC, and Jim Woolsey, marketing man for the American evangelist Jimmy Swaggart. Woolsey had sold his show in 148 countries, including China. As he spun his smooth line in Christian sales talk, John Whale's face was a picture, polite but sublimely unworried by the suggestion that the BBC, in refusing to buy the Jimmy Swaggart telecast, is saying to God that the Gospel isn't very important.

Their discussion was intercut with excerpts from a promotional video, in which Swaggart strutted about with a microphone, waving his finger and shouting about being washed in the blood. British evangelists, too, are making videos in the hope of persuading the networks to show 'more explicit Christian television'. In a pilot called *The Once a Week Show*, a man was seen struggling out of a straitjacket. And you can guess what the point of that was: 'I've discovered as a Christian that Jesus can set me free.'

Spectator 1988

Stomach-Turning

When P.J. Kavanagh expressed the opinion, a few weeks ago, that television critics should review the programmes that people actually watch I was reminded that I must have another go at *Neighbours* (BBC 1) sometime soon. Though I have never got as far as writing about this programme I have frequently taped a whole run of episodes and, somewhat less frequently, forced myself to watch one or two. The challenge was to find some kind of answer to the question, 'Why is *Neighbours* so popular?' Normally, however dreadful the rubbish, I have some inkling as to its appeal. But the popularity of *Neighbours* has remained, for me, an impenetrable mystery.

Last week I taped four episodes and watched three of them. The main plot currently concerns a big bust-up between Scott and Charlene, the young married couple played by Kylie Minogue and Jason Donovan. In real life Minogue and Donovan have both become pop stars. In *Neighbours* they continue to lead lives of stupefying dullness on a horrible modern housing estate. One striking thing about them to a person of my generation is that they show no inclination whatever to get away from their parents. The cause of their quarrel was not existential agony at the prospect of five or six decades of married life in the suburbs but the fact that Charlene saw Scott kissing another girl. Whether the kiss was lustful or brotherly, I cannot tell you. But I do know that Scott is very sorry and wishes Charlene would forgive him. The entire population of the street shares this wish and people talk of little else but their plans to bring Charlene and Scott together again. Male and female, young and old are united in platitudinous concern, observing that all marriages go through rocky patches, and that things have got to be talked through because that's what marriage is all about, mate – communicating with each other.

'It's philosophy, isn't it?' commented the friend who was prevailed upon to keep me company during Friday's episode. 'It ranks with the meditations of Marcus Aurelius. Is that any help? Can I stop watching it now?'

Actually, I think there may be hope for Charlene. She seems genuinely interested in her work as an apprentice garage mechanic. And she responds to all the neighbourly nosiness with healthy irritation. If they push her any harder, perhaps she'll tell them all to go to hell, preferably in foul language, before taking off for the big city and abandoning bourgeois respectability for ever.

Channel 4's screening of *Prick Up Your Ears*, the film about Joe Orton, provided a welcome change. There's nothing like a week of *Neighbours* to enhance one's enjoyment of a homosexual seduction scene that takes place while the television at the end of the bed is broadcasting the Coronation. Or to help one appreciate the scurrilous plot summary, involving a lesbian policewoman, that Orton and his friend Kenneth Halliwell wrote in a library copy of a novel by Dorothy Sayers. Of course, the film will have shocked a few viewers and some scenes were a bit much for me. In one of them Halliwell is preparing supper. 'Do you want rice pudding with the sardines,' he asks, 'or separate?' 'With,' replies Orton. There's a close-up of the unconventional meal and then the two stand side by side at the window, eating it up with relish. Seeing that kind of thing on television, honestly, it turns your stomach.

Spectator 1989

Blame it on the Box

Here is a horrifying statistic, culled from last week's *This Week* (ITV). The typical viewer's television-watching over a year would fill January and February twenty-four hours a day. If I remember rightly, the last horrifying statistic of this kind that came to my attention suggested that the average viewer watched for twenty-seven hours a week. Does the arithmetic tally? If I were less pressed for time, I might be tempted to put the question to a calculator. In any case it is clear that a lot of people are watching far, far more television than can possibly be good for them. How can they be encouraged to watch less? Why isn't there more urgent public debate on this important issue? It would be a good idea to make it the subject of simultaneous two-hour discussion programmes on all four channels, each programme featuring a panel of television executives and politicians. Obviously very few people would want to watch any of these programmes and the rest would have to find something else to do.

Of course, our main concern must be the amount of television watched by young children. Here's a suggestion for parents. Let your children watch whatever they like, on condition they have to write about it afterwards. If my experience is anything to go by, they will soon discover a preference for reading or playing in the fresh air.

BBC 1 has just begun a new experiment in children's broadcasting. It's called *What's Your Story?* and it is presented by a man called Sylvester. Sylvester isn't especially young but he makes up for it by wearing a multicoloured T-shirt under a pink jacket and by dashing round the studio like a hyperactive five-year-old. On Monday afternoon he introduced the first instalment of a serial and the idea is that viewers should decide what happens next. At the end of the episode a boy and a girl (goodies) and a middle-aged man (dressed in a boring green anorak and probably a baddy) were searching a disused mine, where they discovered a newly built brick wall. Back in the studio, rows and rows of telephones were ringing. 'Hello,' said Sylvester. 'Hello, Colin. You think there's a body inside the wall. Thank you very much. That may well be in tomorrow's programme.' Someone else thought the wall concealed special powers that produce mysteries and stuff like that. It reminded me of the Joyce Grenfell sketch in which her nursery teacher learns the pitfalls of asking the children to help make up the story. ('What shall we call our bunny rabbit? No, Hazel, I don't think Princess Anne is a very good name for a bunny rabbit.') But, with twenty-four hours between episodes, the programme-makers will have the opportunity to select sensible suggestions and I'm sure they will make a success of this worthwhile and commendable project.

Of several other programmes I've seen in the last week, the one that proves most memorable is a beautiful and moving documentary called *The Power of Music* (BBC 1). This was about music therapy and it showed practitioners at work with disturbed and handicapped children and adults. It was narrated by Paul McCartney and produced by Ann Paul. The direction and camera-work were superb, with telling shots of hands and faces leaving the viewer in no doubt as to the value of what was going on. In one of the most impressive scenes, a young therapist called Michelle Scott worked with a group of elderly, institutionalised patients in a mental hospital. One of them, Maurice, was very depressed that day and had been reluctant to join the session. Michelle was sensitive with him – there was no offensive jollying-along – and eventually he joined in with her singing. He still didn't look happy, just a little less lost in misery.

The distinguished therapist Dr Clive Robbins explained that it is important to find the right musical mood for each patient. To this end, students in training learn to improvise. In the most joyful scene in the film, a group of students enjoyed a session of improvised singing. It caused me to reflect how sad it is that singing plays such a small part, nowadays, in most people's lives. I blame it on television.

Spectator 1988

Class Struggle

'Teaching brings out the best in people,' says the DES television advertisement. This little film features a French lesson, in which an unseen teacher asks one pupil how old he is. He is *onze*, just turning *douze*. He is charming. While he converses with his teacher, the rest of the class is silent, presumably enthralled by the exchange. There are no paper aeroplanes or scuffles about stolen rubbers to lower the tone of this Department of Education and Science fantasy. No one talks out of turn. No one has to be told off. It may be like that in some schools but potential recruits shouldn't bank on it.

Last week's edition of *Present Imperfect* (BBC 2), entitled *A Teacher's Lot*, looked at Spurley Hey High School in Manchester. We saw some of the staff at work in their classrooms. 'Stop that, Gary. Can we have some quiet in here, please? Can we have some QUIET in here, please?'

'We spend so much time policing,' commented one of them, 'that there's very little over for teaching.'

That's an old problem. Then there are the new ones. How can they meet the demands of the National Curriculum with inadequate funding and facilities? How safe are their jobs? How should they go about marketing the school and attracting support from local businesses? Spurley Hey succeeded in persuading Barclays Bank to produce some folders – complete with Barclays logo – to hand out to local primary schools. The head and one of his staff managed to be moderately enthusiastic about this achievement. Everyone else at the meeting looked depressed and appalled.

'I can't ever remember morale being as low as this,' said a teacher. 'For the first time in seventeen years I didn't want to go back,' said another. If one thing became clear, it was that teaching is not bringing out the best in these people.

For anyone who has been a school teacher, it is a strange experience addressing an audience of polite, silent grown-ups. The grown-ups who had gathered to listen to Alan Bennett talking about Thomas Hardy in *Poetry in Motion* (Channel 4) looked deeply moved and very serious, as poetry audiences usually do. When a poetry event is televised, it is customary to include close-up pictures of one youngish, attractive woman looking especially moved and serious. The woman in question almost always has long, dark hair. She may really be paying attention to the speaker. She may be thinking about her lover or the telephone bill or wondering if she's going to look OK on television. There's no way of knowing.

It's quite likely that the dark-haired woman seen in close-up in *Poetry in Motion* was actually listening to Alan Bennett. His introductions and readings of Hardy's poems were very good. I look forward to hearing him on Housman, Auden and Larkin, even though it will probably mean putting up with more silly bits of film dreamed up by the television people to go with the poems. This is the downside of *Poetry in Motion*. While we were hearing 'In Church', we saw pictures of the inside of a church. At the point where the vestry door opens, the vestry door opened. There's a mirror in the poem, so they put a mirror in the film. It made you feel like a three-year-old being conducted through an alphabet book. I wish they wouldn't do it.

Spectator 1990

A Man's World

'On Wenlock Edge the wood's in trouble.' On screen leaves and branches shook violently in the wind. You got the message: this wood was in very bad trouble. I only hope nobody was hurt while they were out in the gale filming it. They can't have had much fun.

Despite the troubled wood, and despite sound effects (booming guns) to go with 'Epitaph on an Army of Mercenaries', the *Poetry in Motion* programme on A.E. Housman (Channel 4) was better than the one on Hardy the previous week. The moral seems to be: if you don't want television people to do silly things with your poems, write short ones. Several poems were given to us straight, without any pictures at all.

Apart from that little problem, Alan Bennett was, once again, very easy to listen to. His portrait of Housman was intelligent and entertaining. It was a pity he didn't put in any of the funny poems, but a good idea to include Hugh Kingsmill's parody. ('What, still alive at twenty-two?/ A clean, upstanding lad like you?')

One interesting point that Bennett raised was about Housman and women readers. 'I'm not sure that the poems actually appeal to women,' he said. 'Certainly I can't find any woman critic who has written about him.' Housman is very high on my list of favourite poets but, come to think of it, I haven't heard other women enthusing about him. The poet's sister Clemence seems to have enjoyed his work. On first reading *A Shropshire Lad*, she is said to have cried out, with a mixture of sorrow and relief, 'Alfred has a heart!'

Maybe some women readers are put off – as I was for a long time – by the title of Housman's best-known book. If you don't know Shropshire and you've never been a lad, it is uninviting. Some viewers will have noticed that the title misled Channel 4's presentation department. After the end of the Hardy programme we were told that next week's would be about 'the Shropshire lad, A.E. Housman'. A week later, in a pre-programme announcement prefaced by the words 'we're told', he was described as 'a solicitor's son with no rural connections'. That isn't exactly true either – I suspect that an angry memo winged its way to presentation and somewhat overstated its case.

Having devoted a lot of space to poetry two weeks running, I suppose I should try and write about something else next week. You will appreciate that the scope is limited at present. It seems that an important football competition is taking place somewhere in southern Europe. If proof were needed that the world is run for the benefit of men, you need only look at the current television schedules. Of course, as I've said before, it is possible to get interested in almost anything – even football or golf – if you spend enough time gawping at it on the box. But, as Housman frequently reminds us, we tarry here for a very short time. I'm glad I didn't spend any of my allocation watching England and Holland fight it out to a goalless draw.

Spectator 1990

Kind of Weird

At a lunch a little while ago I met a man who is writing a book about philistines. He said I'm in it. Well, I don't mind really, but it did cause me to reflect that it's this wretched column that gives the game away. Other people can be philistine in secret. It's difficult for me to avoid admitting that I didn't see Trevor Nunn's production of *Othello* (BBC 2) because I couldn't bear to miss *thirtysomething* (Channel 4).

The thing is one can reread *Othello* any time but Saturday was the only chance to find out what happened when Hope was seriously tempted to have an affair with her bearded colleague John. Regular viewers will have noticed Hope and John eyeing each other in a way that suggested something more than the mutual respect of keen environmentalists. Last week the campaign they've been involved in ended in failure, and there was no longer any reason for them to meet. She rang him up, wondering 'if maybe that we, you know, didn't explore all of our options'.

The language they use in *thirtysomething* is a big part of the attraction. I found myself imagining what this team of scriptwriters might do with the drama on the other channel: 'Look, guys, I guess some of you maybe have a problem with the idea of me and Desdemona getting together and, like, some of you probably think I'm some kind of hick and maybe you're wondering what this rough old veteran did to pull a chick like her. Well, I want to talk to you about that.'

Hope and John got as far as exploring their options in a Washington hotel room but – as we might have guessed – they decided at the last minute to be strong. Fighting pollution, refraining from adultery, they are a fine example to us all.

If Gertrude Stein had had the opportunity to write a script for *thirtysomething*, it would probably be a bit like this:

Michael and Melissa: We are two cousins.
We had the same grandparents.
We are two cousins.
We had the same grandparents.

Hope and Ellyn: We are not cousins.
We were in high school together.
We are not cousins.
We were in high school together.

Melissa: What shall we do now?

We philistines find it hard to see the point of this kind of thing, or to fathom the significance of lines such as, 'There is no chair here because I am sitting on it.' But, surprisingly, the Dutch production of *Three Plays* by

Gertrude Stein (Channel 4) was tolerable viewing. The main thing it had going for it was very enjoyable music – plinky plonky oriental/avant-garde with a beat – by Fay Lovsky. The composer also did all the voices, recording the words on her soundtrack. So the actors – or dancers – had only to move around and make faces, which they did very well. Furthermore the programme featured some exciting trick camera work. In the last play, entitled *Look and Long*, one character was split in two, one grew very thin, and a third was turned into an egg. And then they were all changed back again by a female conjuror wearing a dog mask.

'Only Heineken can do this,' said the voice-over. No, not really. As they would say in *thirtysomething*, it was kind of weird.

Spectator 1990

Ill-Judged

Is it normal for a Finn to travel with a zip-up case containing eleven toothbrushes? A question like that would only occur to someone who is very bored indeed. The eleven toothbrushes belonged to the central character in a Finnish programme called *Neutral Policy*, one of two items in Sunday's *A Joke Too Far* (Channel 4). It was about a man who stayed in his hotel room while all kinds of dramatic events – an orgy, a murder, a revolution – went on in the world outside. I think it had a political message, but couldn't even begin to guess why it was entered for the Montreux Golden Rose Comedy Award. It didn't win.

The other half of *A Joke Too Far* was a Danish offering entitled *The Søren Kierkegaard Roadshow*. A lorry driver pontificated about life to a younger companion. He told two stories, which were dramatised on the screen. One was about a murder, the other about a rape. Here again, it was difficult to see which bits were supposed to be the jokes.

The average British 'comedy' programme is quite different. It isn't funny but it is packed with lines and incidents that are recognisable as failed attempts at humour. And, now and again, we are agreeably surprised by a successful attempt. On the two occasions when I've seen it, *Drop the Dead Donkey* (Channel 4) has made me laugh, mainly because it panders to some of my worst prejudices about television people. There's Henry (David Swift), the vain, ageing newsreader, who thinks he is God's gift to women. There's Sally (Victoria Wicks), the perfectly groomed pinhead, who has been chosen for her looks. And there's Damien (Stephen Tompkinson), the ambitious young reporter, who knows what he wants and goes out and gets it even if it means buying tins of lager for sober football fans or putting washing-up liquid into cattle-feed so that the cows will foam at the mouth. The editor and producers are portrayed as rather nice, unpretentious people, whose chief fault is a willingness to compromise under pressure from the proprietor. Of course, I don't really believe that television newsrooms are anything like this. My limited experience of television people suggests that news and current affairs producers are tough, brave, honest and, in their own way, every bit as self-important as the personalities who appear on the screen.

The freedom to ignore it all for five weeks has been wonderful. I hardly watched anything except the news, a few times, and *thirtysomething* (until the end of the series – those episodes about the takeover bid were awfully good) and *L.A. Law* (ITV). I found myself discussing the latter programme at a dinner party last week with a man who confessed to being shocked when Grace was made a judge. Why? Because he used to fancy her but he feels that one can't possibly fantasise about having a relationship with a judge. This seemed to me an appalling attitude and I said so at some length, pointing out, as if it clinched the argument, that Michael Kuzak fancies her more since her promotion. My speech attracted the attention of the other guests, most of whom were Californian academics on holiday in London. None of them had ever watched *L.A. Law* for as much as five minutes. One professor just couldn't believe his ears.

'You watch *soaps*?' His amazement was polite, uncensorious and pure.

'I write a column about television,' I explained. Sometimes one is glad of the excuse.

Spectator 1990

The Archers

My father disapproved of *The Archers* – I'm not sure why. We never listened to it at home but I went to boarding school when I was seven and had the programme inflicted on me against my will. This is what happened: our matron used to gather us in her room and read to us before we went to bed. She was in the middle of a book called *The Little Grey Men* when someone suggested we might like to listen to *The Archers* instead. There was a vote. I voted for the book but the radio programme won.

Thereafter we sat down at 6.45 every evening (I think it was 6.45 in those days) and listened to the everyday story of country folk. Quite soon I got interested and looked forward to the next episode. My most vivid memory is of the vet announcing, 'I'm afraid [heavy pause] it's foot and mouth disease.' This news was so appalling that the programme closed with doom-laden chords instead of the usual signature tune. 'What's foot and mouth disease?' we all wanted to know. 'Can people catch it?' Reassured that they couldn't, I felt the music had been a bit over the top.

In the school holidays I didn't miss *The Archers* at

all. It was easy to pick up the story next term because nothing much happened. That's one of the great things about it. In 1999, when I was a regular listener, I spent five weeks in Colorado. When I came back Tom Archer's court case was still going on and everything was much the same as before. Admittedly we did miss the great drama in 1955 when Grace Archer was burnt to death in an attempt to distract attention from the opening of ITV. That occurred in the school holidays. The Cope family was in front of the television, fascinated by the advertisements.

In adult life I've had phases when I listened to *The Archers* every day and phases when I couldn't be bothered. There's a poem in my new book about the programme which begins: 'I like *The Archers* only when it's got/ Adulterous behaviour in the plot.' Sid and Jolene, Brian and Siobhan, Emma and Ed, Ruth and Sam – all of those had me switching on regularly at 7 p.m. Come to think of it, it doesn't necessarily have to be adultery: an unsuitable love affair will do. I remember being riveted by the story of Elizabeth Archer and Cameron Fraser. They were last heard together in a cafe after Elizabeth discovered she was pregnant. Cameron Fraser went to the Gents and never came back. He had climbed out of a window and driven away. Once it was clear that Cameron was a thoroughly bad lot, he was banished from the script, just like the man who beat up Shula and Debbie, and Debbie's errant husband. This annoys me. I think it would be interesting to allow bad characters to stick around for a bit. At least we've still got Matt Crawford to dilute the blandness.

As for the good characters, over the years I have come to like many of them less and less. My number one hate is Jennifer Archer. An intelligent woman, who used to write when she was younger, she now does nothing except cook meals for her family and go on about how much she'd like to have them all home with her for Christmas.

When her daughter Kate announced that she was planning to go to university, Jennifer just couldn't understand it. Kate is married and has children. Why on earth would she want to study for a degree? It's the kind of moment that makes you want to get inside the radio and shake her.

Jennifer's sister Lillian is more likeable but unfortunately I can't forget that Lillian used to be played by a different actress with a different voice. And, as far as I can recall, she was an entirely different character. The programme-makers must have thought they could get away with that but some of us have long memories.

Then there's David. I think we're meant to like and admire David and it has taken some time for me to admit to myself that I don't. He is one of those no-nonsense blokes who tend to be rather impatient with women like me. I'm not crazy about Ruth either, or Jill, and certainly not crazy about Shula, who resembles a bossy head girl. I quite like Kenton and Brian and Elizabeth. Adam and Ian and Debbie are OK too.

And I have a soft spot for Fallon. But my favourite character was Nigel. Nigel, the kindly, patient, devoted husband, was loveable.

They nearly killed him off once before. This was long ago, before he was married. He was a young, amiable upper-class twit, who had an unsuccessful relationship with Shula before he fell for her sister. When news of his imminent demise leaked, listeners protested so much that his life was saved. This time they made sure that no one got a chance to object. When Nigel fell off the roof, I was sure he would survive, perhaps in a wheel-chair. There would be plenty of dramatic mileage in his struggle to come to terms with his terrible injuries. But no. He was dead and there was nothing anyone could do about it.

I am boycotting *The Archers* and, unlike some of my friends, I haven't weakened yet. A couple of weeks ago I met a woman who said her mother had been boycotting the programme ever since Grace Archer died. Completely pointless, of course, but somehow admirable. I'm happy to see that Graham Seed, who played Nigel, has been the subject of several newspaper articles and that he has been making some public appearances around the country. I hope his career will flourish. I hope he will become so rich and famous and sought-after that Vanessa Whitburn will rue the day she deprived him of his employment.

Sunday Telegraph 2011

ACKNOWLEDGMENTS

The Publishers would like to thank the following:

Rachel Foss, Lead Curator, Modern Literary Manuscripts at the British Library and the staff of the Reading Room, for all their help in putting this book together.

Thanks for editorial help to Tara Gladden, Martin Bryant and Celia Levett, and to Jon McNaught for his wonderful illustrations.

PERMISSIONS

Wendy Cope's prose pieces have previously appeared in the following publications:

Areté, *Bookcase*, *The Compleet Molesworth* (Folio Society), *Daily Mail*, *Daily Telegraph*, *The Dark Horse*, *Dream Catcher*, *The Epic Poise: A Celebration of Ted Hughes* (Faber), Faber & Faber catalogue, *Guardian*, *George Herbert: verse and prose* (SPCK), *How To Write Poetry* (Guardian), *Icons of England* (Think Books/CPRE), *Independent*, Institute of Psychoanalysis news, Kingston University website, *Listener*, *Modern Delight* (Waterstones/Faber), Poetry Book Society bulletin, Poetry Society newsletter, *Spectator*, *The Times*, *Times Educational*

Supplement, Waterstones Magazine, Wykeham Life.

Daddy Played 'Chopsticks' was a talk broadcast on Radio 3. *Battle for Artistic Autonomy* was a speech delivered at the Battle of Ideas.

Grateful acknowledgment is made to the following for permission to reprint previously published material:

Faber & Faber Ltd: *The Iron Man, How the Whale Became and other stories* and 'Moon-Hops', copyright © Ted Hughes. Reprinted by permission of Faber & Faber Ltd, on behalf of the Estate of Ted Hughes.

Every reasonable effort has been made to trace the copyright holders, but if there are any errors or omissions, Two Roads will be pleased to insert the appropriate acknowledgment in any subsequent printing or editions.

ABOUT THE AUTHOR

Wendy Cope read history at Oxford and then worked for fifteen years as a London primary school teacher. Her first book of poems, *Making Cocoa for Kingsley Amis,* was published in 1986. Since then she has been a freelance writer. Her most recent book of poems is *Family Values*, published in 2011. She lives in Ely.

TWO ROADS

Stories . . . voices . . . places . . . lives

We hope you enjoyed *Life, Love and The Archers*. If you'd like to know more about this book or any other title on our list, please go to www.tworoadsbooks.com

For news on forthcoming Two Roads titles, please sign up for our newsletter.

enquiries@tworoadsbooks.com

TwoRoadsBooks